BOOKSTOCK
MANAGEMENT
IN PUBLIC
LIBRARIES

BOOKSTOCK MANAGEMENT IN PUBLIC LIBRARIES

TONY HOUGHTON
Chairman, Public Sector Management Ltd

Foreword by MICHAEL ASSER
County Librarian of Berkshire

CLIVE BINGLEY LONDON

British Library Cataloguing in Publication Data

Houghton, Tony
   Bookstock management in public libraries.
   1. Public libraries—Collection development
   I. Title
   025.2   Z687

ISBN 0 85157 387 8

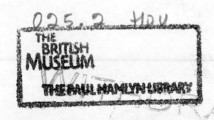

Contents

Foreword

I am privileged to have been asked to contribute a foreword to *Bookstock Management.*

This book is timely; for almost a decade libraries have been living with the consequences of economic recession. Declining book funds predicate increasing restrictions on the range of bookstock provided in libraries. Coming so soon after the boom years of the sixties it is no wonder that the response of librarians to the pressures of a contracting resource base were often ill-thought out, ad hoc and contradictory. There were exceptions. Three years after local government reorganization Alex Wilson, then Director of Libraries in Cheshire, was addressing several of the questions raised in the present book in his paper 'The Threshold of Choice', to the Public Libraries Group Weekend School. The seminal Hillingdon Report related library provision to community need in a very precise way. Tony Houghton's work thus takes its place with the research that has been done throughout the past seven or eight years. This is a book that has come out of hard times; a book for hard times certainly. But if it were no more than that it would not possess enduring value. The significance of the present work is that the principles embodied in it are equally applicable to good times.

Tony Houghton states the object of the book succinctly: to help provide a better quality of service to the borrower. With this goes the contention, unquestionable surely, that a better quality of service is brought about by better understanding based upon measurement and analysis. A proper understanding of the way in which lending libraries function is essential to ensure that the best is obtained from limited resources. All librarians would at least pay lip service to this.

Nevertheless it is fair to say that librarians are still generally more comfortable with the tasks associated with the acquisition and recording of stock than those concerned with monitoring its performance.

It is obvious that the popularity of a book, even a popular book, is not static, but declines fairly rapidly towards the end of its shelf life. Tony Houghton makes the point that the quality of a shelf stock is more important than its size: whether there is a good range of choice and whether the most popular books are adequately represented. The measure of demand by the number of books loaned from a library is convenient and attractive to librarians, but it is always related to the supply of books and issues can always be increased by the purchase of new stock. What is needed is a measure of demand that is independent of supply. A crucial element of the author's research is his concern to establish a formula for gauging the popularity of a bookstock that is a supply-free measure of demand. The bookstock replacement levels necessary to maintain supply targets are themselves targets for the librarians to adhere to. This is a new concept in the job of book selection and acquisition. The author believes that it is no longer enough to scan publishers' lists and select from the 'good' books. It is necessary to ask further questions — is the book necessary to meet the targets, and is it a good buy in terms of the number of issues that it will achieve? There is a trade-off at this stage between the desire of the librarian to see a high-quality stock in the library and the expressed demand of the reading public.

It is important to remember that Tony Houghton is insistent that what is here being offered to librarians is a *tool*, a tool that can be applied impartially to varying circumstances. The application of this tool will always be conditioned by subjective judgement and prevailing local policies and conditions. It does not inevitably entail a reduction in the size of stock or in the choice offered. What it does mean is that the reason for every book's tenure of the shelves can be clearly identified. Certainly application of Tony Houghton's ideas in the foreseeable future is likely to be towards 'doing more with less'. Even as I write, two library authorities have made the national headlines following savage reductions in their book funds.

In summary, the real importance of this book is that it

seeks to replace the subjective, impressionistic assessment of how a book works during its life on the library shelves by a proper analysis, resulting in a formula-based approach which can be applied with confidence to varying circumstances. Applied common sense? Yes, but common sense which can be justified before elected members and the like who sit in judgement upon the public library service. This is a noteworthy addition to the research into bookstock management in libraries and deserves close study by all librarians concerned with the management of resources and the proper application of public funds.

Michael Asser
County Librarian of Berkshire

Acknowledgements

My interest in public libraries and library research stems from my research work done for the British Library over a period of years. I would like to acknowledge the support and assistance I have received from a succession of project officers but especially Nick Moore and Sue Howley.

There are a number of librarians working on various aspects of systematic bookstock management and this book has been influenced by their work. In particular, this book would not have been possible without the stimulus I have received in numerous discussions with Doug Betts of the Surrey County Library Service.

The examples used in this book are drawn from recent research carried out in Berkshire and I would like to thank the County Librarian, Mike Asser, and Branch Librarian, Mary Nance, for their cooperation. I would also like to acknowledge the assistance of my colleagues in Public Sector Management Ltd.

Recently Nick Moore appeared in another guise as commissioning editor for this book. He read through the manuscript as a typical 'innumerate librarian'. If this book remains opaque in parts the blame is entirely mine.

I would like to thank Sue Brind for typing the manuscript and my wife for arranging two holiday cottages for me to take myself away to and write.

Chapter One

Introduction

This book is written for librarians by a library user. The book is intended to help public librarians provide a better quality of service to the borrowers. It is written from a 'systems' viewpoint. Underlying the book is the belief that a higher quality of service will be brought about by a better understanding based on measurement and analysis.

The need for this book is evident. The sixties were a period of growth. This growth was enjoyed by the public sector and public libraries obtained their fair share of resources. Book funds increased steadily year by year and as a consequence the stock of libraries seemed better able to meet the demands placed upon it. The sorts of difficult decisions that librarians then faced concerned the acquisition of expensive specialist books and the number of multiple copies of more popular works which they should buy.

There was a tendency to view each branch library as an independent unit and to work towards a well-balanced stock in each service point, relying on the existence of the rest of the library system to meet the needs for specialist material.

The cuts in expenditure in recent years have hit public library systems particularly badly. Librarians were not well equipped to stretch increasingly scarce resources in such a way that the demands placed upon the service could continue to be met. The popular recreational use of libraries was especially badly hit as cuts were applied pro rata across all the libraries in the system and across the entire bookstock within each library. The effect was to move from a situation which was tolerable for the average borrower to one that was clearly not.

The reduced choice available to borrowers produced a

reduction in use and a fall in issues. Readers with specialist interests also suffered with a curtailment of the range and depth of material acquired. Further problems arose with the increased charges for reservations and inter-library lending.

This book does not suggest that any of these problems can be resolved by arithmetic. Nevertheless a proper understanding of the way in which lending libraries work based on information and analysis is essential to ensure that the best is obtained from limited resources. What the best is, however, will always be a matter for value judgement and policy decision. Some librarians will decide to spend their limited resources on providing a service for the specialist borrower and on meeting educational needs. Others will attempt to provide a balanced service with material to suit all tastes. A third group will concentrate on catering for mass demand in the hope that by enlisting the support of the electorate in this way further cuts can be avoided. The point is that to pursue any of these policies effectively calls for an understanding of the dynamics of the library and some basic management information.

This book is divided into two parts. The first part, consisting of chapters 2 to 5 inclusive, provides a basic theoretical background. The remainder, and the bulk, of the book describes specific techniques for putting the theory into practice by measuring and analysing library performance and using this information to formulate and evaluate policy.

The next chapter (2) describes the context in which the librarian is working and defines the types of libraries that are covered by the treatment in this book. This is followed by a substantial chapter (3) on the theory of book circulation. This theory must be understood as it is the basis for the arguments presented in the entire book. The theory is used in chapter 4 to work up some techniques for measuring the performance of the library and the bookstock within it. The economic principles of supply and demand are used as a basis for performance measurement. Finally, the first part of the book concludes with chapter 5, which outlines some of the policy options open to the librarian. A distinction is made between those policies that are necessary immediately in order to get a library back on the rails and achieving its targets, and those policies which are longer term, concerned with maintaining a library that meets the targets that have been set for it.

Chapter 6 opens the second part of the book with an outline of the systematic approach to library management. Broadly, this approach consists of three stages: survey, analysis and plan. The need for information can be supplied in part by records already kept in the library. This preliminary assessment is described in chapter 7 as a prelude to special surveys which may be carried out in a library or group of libraries. In chapter 8 the technique for these surveys is set out in some detail and includes sampling and questionnaire design as well as the techniques for actually conducting the survey.

There are two chapters on analysis. The first (9) is concerned with the process of assembling data from the various surveys and ensuring that the data obtained from various sources are consistent and represent reality. This chapter includes a description of techniques for analysing sample surveys so that a picture of the whole stock can be built up. This is followed by a chapter (10) in which the techniques for expanding the data base are described. At the end of this chapter a data matrix will have been built up which describes the performance of all the groups of books in a library. Such data can be misleading, especially if the library is not in a state of stable equilibrium. Chapter 11 discusses the way in which the data should be interpreted to give an accurate picture of the performance of a library on which policies for change can be based. The idea of targets for policy is also introduced at this stage.

Chapters 12 to 14 are concerned with policy matters. First (in 12) we discuss the effects of restructuring the bookstock by reclassification, injecting and weeding stock as a means of achieving targets. We then describe (in 13) a policy that is particularly suited to the treatment of low-interest books in small libraries, namely bookstock rotation. These two chapters have described one-off policies aimed at achieving targets. Chapter 14 goes on to show how those targets can be maintained by consistent replacement and withdrawal policies.

Analysis must not be considered as a one-off exercise designed to meet a short-term need. Rather, it should be a way of managing libraries on a continuing basis. To achieve this it is necessary to set up a monitoring process. This process is described in chapter 15. Many of the ideas introduced in this book will have profound organizational implications. The quality and placement of staff will need to be reviewed and the structure of the library system may need to be adapted to capitalize on the benefits to be obtained from this approach. These implications are discussed in chapter 16.

The techniques described in chapters 7 to 15 are complex. Moreover, there is a range of alternatives from which the correct technique may be selected only after a detailed examination of the circumstances of a particular library system. Nevertheless, in an attempt to simplify this analytical process, chapter 17 gives a 'cookbook' of techniques that should provide a useful summary to the librarian who is about to embark on a systematic review of a library service.

Chapter Two

The Library

In this book we are primarily concerned with the public lending library service. Academic libraries are not covered specifically, nor are the non-lending services offered by public library systems such as the reference service and other information services. Throughout we will refer to books and bookstock. However, the ideas and techniques discussed are equally appropriate to other material which is lent by public lending libraries, such as gramophone records and videos. Most of the illustrations used in this book are for an adult lending library providing a range of books, both fiction and non-fiction. There is no specific discussion of the special problems of providing a library service for junior readers although, again, the techniques described can be applied.

In a typical lending library the borrower will make a selection of books from the shelf. There will be a maximum limit to the number of books that can be withdrawn at any one time by a borrower. Sometimes this maximum will be further subdivided with limits placed on both fiction and non-fiction books.

The shelf stock of the library will be displayed in some sort of order. Many libraries have adopted the Dewey decimal system of book classification which orders the books into a rational hierarchical structure. The Dewey system is appropriate only to non-fiction books and therefore fiction is usually displayed in alphabetical order, according to author. This method of book grouping, though rational, does not necessarily correspond to reader interest categories; for example, railway books might be shelved under engineering or transport. To add to the problems of using a library of this type, the librarian responsible for acquiring and shelving the books may not be sufficiently familiar with the subject of a book to place it under the right classification. The A to Z classification of fiction does not help the reader who has read a good book and wishes to borrow another one similar but not necessarily by the same author.

To overcome these problems some libraries are experimenting with shelving the books in reader interest categories. Thus, the railway book, whether it is specifically biased towards engineering or a more general treatment of the subject, would be shelved under some broad category such as transport. Fiction is dealt with by shelving it under genre groupings such as Mystery, Romance, Science Fiction, Short Stories, etc. As we will see later, a categorized library works best when there are a limited number of categories of about the same size. The purpose of categorization will be destroyed if there are too many miscellaneous or ill-defined categories. This requirement presents grave difficulties to the librarian who is trying to categorize a library. Later in this book we will talk of categories in relation to data collection and analysis. It is important to realize that these survey categories do not necessarily correspond to categories which may be used for display purposes.

Once the borrower has selected the book from the shelf he will present it to the library assistant for issuing. There are a number of issuing systems currently in use in public libraries, ranging from a token system where the borrower exchanges a plastic token for a book, through to more sophisticated computerized issuing systems where the details of the reader and the book being borrowed are recorded on a central computer file. Most libraries impose a maximum loan period on the borrower and this information is given in the form of a date stamp in the book at the time that the book is issued.

This simple self-service procedure adopted by most borrowers in public libraries is usually supplemented by other aids to the borrower. Most libraries have a catalogue that is designed to help borrowers find particular books in areas in which they are interested. This catalogue will certainly show all the details of the books currently belonging to the library and it may also give details of books in the same library system but belonging to other libraries. The catalogue will therefore provide a wider choice than the books displayed on the shelves. The librarian is also available in most libraries to help borrowers with their book selection and often the catalogue will be used as a source of reference for this service.

To supplement the choice of books from the shelf most libraries offer a reservation service to enable users to borrow books that may be part of the library's stock but which are not currently displayed. This reservation service can also be used by the borrower to reserve books not in the library's catalogue but which may be held by another library or in some central store. Inter-library lending is also supplemented by a large stock of non-fiction books held by the British Library Lending Division at Boston Spa, Yorkshire, as well as more local cooperative arrangements between systems. The costs of the reservation and inter-library lending services are not insignificant and in these days of financial stringency their use is effectively discouraged by librarians who levy substantial fees on the borrower for them.

The borrower entering the library therefore has a choice of picking a book from the shelf or reserving a particular title that is not currently available in the library. Faced with the costs and the delay involved in adopting the second option, the vast majority of borrowers select their reading material from the shelf. As this is the case it is important that libraries are designed principally around this method of borrowing. The job of the librarian should be to ensure that there is an adequate choice of books on the shelf from which the borrower can make a selection. This may seem a daunting task, especially in those areas of popular demand where it may appear to the librarian that the shelf stock is constantly depleted by the depredations of borrowers who take the books out on loan. Nevertheless, we will show in this book that even in these categories of books an adequate shelf stock can be maintained.

This concentration on providing a choice on the shelf does not mean that the library should be dealt with in isolation from other libraries in the system. Inter-library lending will be an important, though minority, activity within the library service, but more importantly we will show later that individual libraries within a system can provide a livelier stock of books more cost-effectively by sharing their stock with other libraries in the form of circulating collections.

Before we move on to an investigation of the behaviour of the bookstock in a lending library it is worth looking at two general policy issues. These are the maximum number of books that a borrower can borrow and the maximum loan period imposed on him. In recent years there has been a tendency to allow borrowers to take more books from the library for longer periods. This policy certainly means that the borrower need make fewer visits to the library each year and there may be a small saving in the library assistant's time in issuing and discharging books. However, it may lead to borrowers taking more books out of the library than they actually want to read, thus restricting the choice of other borrowers. A longer loan period, when applied to individual books, means that either they are borrowed by fewer people before they are withdrawn, or their life has to be prolonged beyond the point at which they are topical to allow everybody that so wishes to read them. A shorter loan period allows individual books to work much harder and, therefore, yield better value for money.

Chapter Three

Book behaviour

A public lending library service is concerned with the borrower and hence librarians should be interested in and respond to borrower behaviour. Nevertheless, as we will see in succeeding chapters, it is easier to measure what is happening to the books and from this to deduce borrower behaviour, demand and requirements.

To make this step between book behaviour and borrower behaviour we need a theory connecting the two. This theory will be derived from an analysis of how libraries are used by borrowers and how this usage leads to a pattern of book behaviour.

People entering a lending library behave in a variety of ways. There is at least one old gentleman who enters the library, starts at the first book on the shelf immediately inside the door and systematically scans the entire shelf stock of the library before making a choice. Most borrowers have neither the time nor the inclination to adopt this approach and therefore take short cuts. The library may or may not be adapted to facilitate these short cuts but nevertheless most borrowers restrict their choosing of books to a few familiar parts of the library. Whatever the initial approach, borrowing usually involves some sort of choice from a range of books presented on shelves. Few borrowers enter a library with a reading list of specific titles and few consult the catalogue before making a choice. Most borrowers' choice is therefore between a number of books presented to them on the shelves.

In making this choice borrowers will adopt some sort of ranking system. This system may well be in two stages. First, they will reject those books in which they are not at all

interested, and second, they will order the remainder and
select the one with the highest rank. In ranking books there
will be a number of subjective factors that will come into
play. Is it a familiar author? Has it been recommended by
someone? Is it attractively packaged or displayed? Are there
interesting pictures in it? Does the synopsis or the opening
words make it sound exciting? Have they read it before?
Whatever combination of factors influences the borrowers'
choice a choice will be made. This model of borrower behaviour is a thoeretical one but probably not too far from the
truth and a useful basis on which to build.

The borrowers' choice is restricted to those books displayed on the shelf. They cannot select a book that is not
there — if it is out on loan for example. True, some borrowers
will reserve books but this represents a very small proportion
of total issues and is not worth introducing into the analysis.

Borrowers will borrow a particular book as a result of two
factors, therefore. First, is the book available, and second, of
all the group that is available, is it their first choice?

We can examine this concept of book ranking a little
further. Every book in the library has a number of people
interested in it. True, it may not be the first choice for all of
them but they certainly will not reject it. Some books are
very popular and nearly everyone in the library is interested
in reading them. Other books will appeal only to a small
number of people. The more popular the book, that is the
more people interested in it, the greater the chance that it
will be a particular borrower's first choice and, therefore, if
it is available, that it will be borrowed.

The availability of a book is more readily comprehensible.
If it is on the shelf it is available and if it is absent then it is
not available. There is, however, an inter-relationship between popularity and availability. The more popular the
book the greater the chance of it being borrowed and,
therefore, the lower its availability. This inter-relationship
will reach an equilibrium level for each book and this level
will determine the rate at which the book is issued.

Before we can take the analysis further we must introduce
and understand the basics of probability theory. If we were to
toss an unweighted coin it would come down with either
heads or tails uppermost. We can assign a probability to
either event. This probability will be 0·5. In colloquial terms

there is a 50 per cent chance of it falling with either face uppermost. Probabilities can be combined. If we were to toss two coins we can calculate the probability of getting two heads. We do this by multiplying the two component probabilities together. Thus, the probability of getting two heads is 0·5 × 0·5 or 0·25. That is, there is a 25 per cent chance of getting two heads each time the two coins are tossed.

There is an affinity between probabilities and proportions. If we were to toss a coin a large number of times and record the face exposed each time, we would find that after a number of throws a pattern would emerge in which half the throws were heads and the other half tails. That is, the proportion of heads thrown will equal the probability that a head is thrown each time.

We can now apply probability theory to book behaviour. We have argued that the choice of a book by a borrower is dependent on the popularity of the book and its availability. Both these concepts can be expressed in terms of probabilities.

The popularity of a book can be expressed as the probability that a borrower is interested in it. This is the same as the proportion of borrowers interested in the book. Thus, if 50 per cent of the borrowers in a library were interested in reading a particular book, the probability that an individual borrower is interested in it would be 0·5. The ranking that a borrower puts on the book is related to the probability. This relationship is a direct one and can be expressed as follows:

The probability that a book is a borrower's first choice and will be borrowed	=	Constant	×	The probability that the borrower is interested in the book

The constant will always be less than one.

The availability of a book is the probability that a book is on the shelf. This is equal to the proportion of books on the shelf. If we have a group or category of books that are shelved together, each behaving in much the same sort of way, then we can measure the probability that a book in the category is on the shelf by dividing the number of books on the shelf by the total stock in the category.

The two probabilities can be combined to give the probability that a book is borrowed:

The probability that a book is borrowed by a particular borrower	=	The probability that it is on the shelf	X	The probability that it is the borrower's first choice

When a book is borrowed by a particular borrower it represents a borrowing occasion. The sum of such occasions for the library as a whole over a year represents the total annual issues for the library and the sum over a year for the book represents the annual issues of the book. The probability that a book is borrowed is the same as the proportion of the total issues of the library represented by issues of the book, or the annual issues of the book divided by the annual issues of the library.

However, the availability of the book is also a function of its annual issues. This means that we have an equation in which the annual issues of a book, or its circulation, appears on both sides. If we can rearrange this equation we should be able to get a relationship between book circulation and a number of parameters. To do this we have to resort to some algebra.

First, we will define our variables:

n = The probability that the borrower is interested in the book.

p = The probability that the borrower will rank the book as his first choice.

k = A constant.

a = The availability of the book, that is, the probability that it is on the shelf.

I = Annual issues from the library.

C = Annual issues of the book.

We can now rewrite the equations that we have derived in algebraic form:

$$p = kn$$

$$\frac{C}{I} = ap = akn$$

so $$C = aIkn$$

Now let us look at the relationship between availability and book circulation. The probability that a book is on the shelf is one minus the probability that a book is on loan. The probability that a book is on loan is the same as the proportion of time that it spends on loan. Thus, if a book is issued twelve times in a year and each time it is issued it spends on average twenty days out of the library, then it is out of the library for 240 days out of 365. That is, the proportion of time it is out on loan is $240/365 = 0.66$. This is the probability that the book is out on loan.

So if

L = average loan period

then

$$a = 1 - \frac{CL}{365}$$

We can put this back into our equation for C to give

$$C = Ikn\left(1 - \frac{CL}{365}\right)$$

Bringing together the terms in C and simplifying we get

$$C = \frac{365}{L\left(1 + \frac{365}{LIkn}\right)}$$

There is one further simplification we can carry out on this equation. If we look at the term $365/L$ we can see that this represents the number of times that the year can be divided by the average loan period of the book. That is, it is the maximum circulation that a book can achieve if it goes out of the library immediately it is returned. If we call this variable C_{max} we get the equation:

$$C = \frac{C_{max}}{1 + \frac{C_{max}}{Ikn}}$$

For a particular book in a library I and k will be constants for the library and Cmax will be a constant for the group of books containing the particular book. There is, therefore, a direct relationship between the annual issues of a book and the proportion of the borrowers of the library that is interested in reading it. We can tabulate this relationship for typical values of C_{max}, I and k and a range of values of n as follows:

C_{max} = 18·25
I   = 200,000
k   = 0·00037

n	C
0	0
0·1	5·2
0·2	8·1
0·3	10·0
0·4	11·2
0·5	12·2
0·6	12·9
0·7	13·4
0·8	13·9
0·9	14·2
1·0	14·6

From this example we can see clearly the relationship between the circulation of a book and the number of people interested in it. One feature of the relationship is that no matter how great the proportion of people interested in a book (and it cannot exceed 1) the circulation of the book will not exceed the maximum circulation defined by the loan period.

The constant k is worth discussing further before moving on to other things. This is the relationship between the probability that a borrower is interested in a book and the probability that it will be ranked as a first choice. The value of k is related to the range of choice available to the borrower. In the extreme case where the borrower has no choice, then k will be equal to 1 because the probability that the borrower is interested will be the same as the probability that the book will be the first (and only) choice. In practical cases k will be always less than 1 and is in fact inversely proportional to the quality of the library, that is, the range of choice available to the borrower. The greater the range of choice, and hence the higher the quality of the library, the lower will be the value of k.

The popularity of a book, that is, the number of people interested in it and therefore the probability that people are interested, is not static over time. It will tend to decrease for two reasons. The first of these reasons is that people will simply lose interest in the book over time. That is, the probability of a borrower being interested in the book in one year will be a fraction of the probablity in the previous year. This decay in interest will continue. The rate at which the popularity of a book decreases with time will vary between different types of book. Some books wlll remain topical for a long period and therefore their popularity will decline slowly. Other books will lose their topicality more quickly and this will be reflected in a rapid decrease in interest and, hence, circulation.

The second reason for the decline in interest is that once books have been read people are less interested in reading them again. If the circulation of a book in its first year is twelve issues this represents twelve people who are unlikely to want to read the book again. This will be translated into a reduction in the probability that a borrower is interested in the book and, hence, a reduction in its circulation in the second year.

These factors can be combined with the relationship we have derived for the circulation of a book to give us a model for the year-by-year circulation of a book. This relationship depends on two key variables. The first of these is the popularity of the book, that is, the probability that a borrower is interested in it. The second is the rate at which this popularity declines with time. By varying these key variables and plotting the resultant circulation figures on a graph of issues against time a range of circulation curves can be drawn (Figures 1 and 2). We can see broadly speaking that the popularity of the book is related to its initial circulation and the rate of decrease of this popularity (r) governs the way in which the circulation declines with time.

If we have a non-fiction title that appeals to a relatively small readership but whose interest will not flag with time, then we would expect the circulation curve to have a relatively modest initial circulation but thereafter the fall-off in issues to be a function only of the fact that people have read the book and so be relatively slow. On the other hand if we have a popular but topical book in which people lose interest quickly, we would expect it to have a high initial circulation with a fairly rapid fall-off.

In this chapter we have predicted the circulation curve of a book from a knowledge of the characteristics of the book. However, in practice we could do the reverse, that is, deduce the characteristics of the book from its circulation curve.

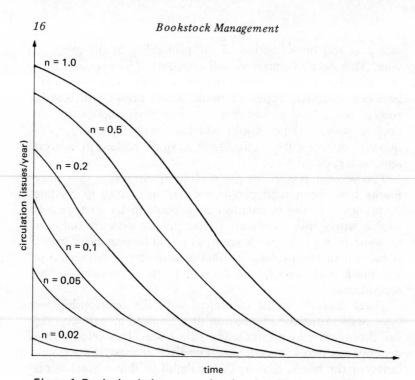

Figure 1 Book circulation curves showing the effect of variations in popularity (n)

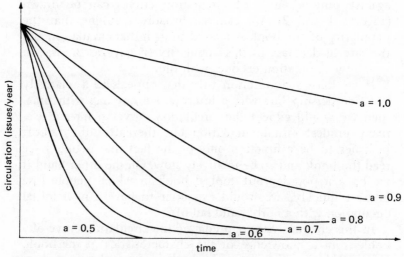

Figure 2 Book circulation curves showing the effect of a decline in popularity with time (a)

We will show in later chapters how circulation curves for books can be built up from data and how an understanding of what these curves mean can be used in building policy.

Chapter Four

Performance measurement

It should be possible to use the theory of borrower and book behaviour, described in the previous chapter, to measure the performance of a lending library and the bookstock within it. A lending library after all is only a means of delivering a commodity to consumers in pretty much the same sort of way as a supermarket. So it should be governed by the same economic laws of supply and demand. We will, therefore, try to measure the performance of a library in these terms. In addition to supply and demand we would like to know a little bit more about the performance of the commodity, that is, the bookstock. Finally, we will take a look at those policies currently in operation in the library and see how successfully demand and supply are matched and how efficiently the bookstock is being used.

When borrowers enter a library they are presented with a choice. This choice is the supply. The choice presented to borrowers is not the entire stock of books in the library because a good proportion of this stock will be out on loan. Instead, borrowers will be able to choose only from the shelf stock. In other words, it is the stock on the shelves that serves the same supply function as the goods on the supermarket shelf. In the previous chapter we saw how the most popular books in the library are the ones that are borrowed most frequently, and therefore spend most of their time on loan. This often means that the shelf stock in a library contains the less popular books that people do not wish to borrow. We should be concerned not only with the size of the shelf stock but with its quality. That is, whether it represents a good range of choice and whether the most popular types of books are adequately represented.

Demand is a difficult concept to measure. In some respects the number of issues from the library is an attractive measure of the demand for the books. However, this measure is inter-related to the supply of books. As we will show later, the issues in a library can always be increased by injecting new stock.What we need is a measure of demand that is independent of supply.

In the previous chapter we based the circulation of a book on the concept of its popularity, that is, the probability that a borrower is interested in it. This concept provides a useful, supply-free, measure of demand. The popularity of a book cannot be measured directly. Surveys of borrowers asking them if they are interested in a particular book, or which books they are interested in, are liable to produce silly results. However, popularity can be measured indirectly by using the relationship we derived in the previous chapter between popularity and book circulation. We can transpose this relationship to get a formula for the popularity of a book in terms of its annual circulation.

The relationship derived in the previous chapter was:

$$C = \frac{C_{max}}{1 + \dfrac{C_{max}}{Ikn}}$$

where

C   is the annual issues of a book,
C_{max} is the maximum annual issues that the book can achieve if it is always on loan (it is equal to the days in the year divided by the average loan period),
I   is the total annual issues from the library,
k   is a constant,
n   is the popularity of the book.

This equation can be rewritten as

$$n = \frac{C_{max}}{Ik} \times \frac{C/C_{max}}{1 - C/C_{max}}$$

This can be simplified in two ways. C_{max}, the constant k and the total issues for the library I will be constant for all books in a library. So if we simply want to compare books in the library we can replace the first term in the formula above by a single constant, or if we want an index of demand we can dispense with it altogether.

The other simplification arises from an examination of the term C/C_{max}. In the previous chapter we defined the probability that a book is on loan as the same as the proportion of time that it spends on loan. This gives us the relationship:

$$\text{Probability that a book is on loan} = \frac{\text{Annual issues of book} \times \text{Loan period}}{365}$$

but the $\dfrac{\text{Loan period}}{365}$ is C_{max}

so the expression C/C_{max} is the probability that a book is on loan. $1 - C/C_{max}$ is the probability that a book is on the shelf. Thus, we have a key relationship:

$$\text{Index of demand} = \frac{\text{Probability that a book is on loan}}{\text{Probability that a book is on shelf}}$$

Both the probabilities can be calculated for individual books provided the annual circulation and the loan period are known. An index of demand can also be calculated for groups of books of roughly similar characteristics by measuring the proportions of books on loan and on the shelf.

The shelf stock is directly related to the stock on loan. If we are interested in ranking books in order of demand, then the relative values of the probability that the book is on loan will be sufficient. If we have two books, one of which spends 80 per cent of its time on loan and the other spends only 20 per cent of its time on loan, then the demand for the first book is greater than the demand for the second. Similarly, if we have two groups of books where 80 per cent of the first group are out on loan at any time and only 20 per cent of the latter, then the demand for books in the first group is higher than the demand for books in the second.

One word of caution needs to be injected in relation to the index of demand defined above. There are two ways of calculating this index for a group of books. The first way is the one described above, namely dividing the proportion on loan by the proportion on the shelf. The second way involves calculating the index separately for each book in the group from the annual circulation of each book and then taking the average. Unless the annual circulation of all the books in the group is the same these two measures will be different. The demand index for a group of books can easily mask significant differences within the group and should, therefore, be interpreted with care. Ideally book groups should be so defined that those differences are small. However, as we have seen, there is a significant difference in the circulation of, and hence demand for, a single book over its lifetime. Altogether it is best to restrict the use of the demand index to individual books or the 'typical' book in a group.

In the previous chapter we saw how the circulation curve of a book represented its 'signature'. It is a guide to those characteristics of a book which will influence its performance in a library. A theoretical circulation curve can be drawn based on two key parameters, the popularity of a book and the rate of decline of popularity over time. In practice it is difficult to estimate these parameters. Actual circulation curves of current books can be derived by plotting the year-by-year circulation on a graph. A typical circulation curve plotted in this way is shown in Figure 3.

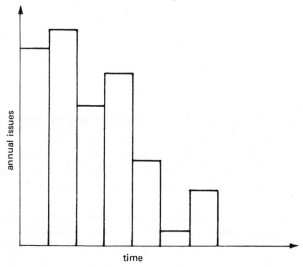

Figure 3 Circulation curve for a typical book

This type of circulation curve is very different from the elegant smooth line that we obtained theoretically. Nevertheless, it still retains many of the important features. It has a relatively high initial circulation which declines more or less to a low residual level before the book is withdrawn. We can obtain a smoother circulation curve by taking a group of books with more-or-less similar characteristics. If we plot the average year-by-year circulation of this group on a similar graph we would get a picture like Figure 4.

This curve is rather more akin to the theoretical curve that we produced earlier. These circulation curves can be described by a number of parameters. The period of time

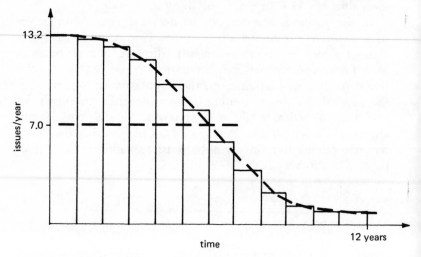

Figure 4 Circulation curve for a group of books

during which the book is circulating in the library, that is, the life of the book, is an obvious parameter. The typical book represented by the curve above has a life of 12 years. The initial circulation of the book is a useful guide to its popularity when new. This can also be measured from the graph and in this case is 13·2.

A book in a library represents an investment by the library system and the return on that investment is measured by the number of issues that the book will achieve in its lifetime. This measure is obtained by adding up the year-by-year circulation of the book. Another way of calculating the total issues is to measure the area under the curve. In both cases we obtain a value of 84 issues from our example. Finally, we can calculate the average annual issues of the book by dividing the total issues by its life. This value is illustrated on the graph and is calculated as 84/12 or 7 issues per year.

All the analysis of circulation curves will be carried out on books that are current in the library or books that have been withdrawn. What we are really interested in, however, is the contribution possible new books will make to the library. It would be useful to know before purchasing a book how many issues it will achieve. This prediction can only be made by a lot of analysis of the existing bookstock so that parallels can be drawn between new books and books that are already in the system.

The librarian will have two objectives: first, to acquire those books that will contribute most to the library in the form of issue potential and second, to maximize the issues of those books already in the library.

Getting the most out of books will not be achieved by wishful thinking. One obvious way to achieve the result is to select for the library only books that are known to have a high degree of popularity and will therefore achieve high total issues. If this policy is pursued over any length of time an unbalanced stock will result with the library containing only popular works. While this may be good for the majority of the borrowers it will leave the specialist borrower and the librarian unhappy. Total issues from each book in a library can be raised by restricting the choice of books, thus forcing the borrower to use the small stock that remains. Although this policy may succeed in the short term it will certainly be counter-productive in the longer term. The restricted choice of books will force people to leave the library, there will be fewer issues from the library as a whole and the issues obtained from individual books may be even lower than before.

There are ways of increasing the total issues of unpopular books and these will be described later in the book.

Managing a library consists of ensuring that the supply of books keeps pace with the demand. To achieve this the principal management technique employed is bookstock replacement. In simple terms this consists of withdrawing books from the library when they have stopped circulating or when they become worn out and replacing them with new books of a similar nature. This approach is fine provided the demand for books remains stable over time and provided due allowance is made in acquiring new books for those that have been lost or stolen from the library. However, if demand for a group of books starts to rise, then replacement can easily fall behind the demand and the books are then put under increasing pressure by the borrowers.

In order to keep pace with the use of books made by the borrowers it is necessary to put back into the library in the form of potential issues of new books what is being taken out by the borrowers. This means that the sum of the potential issues injected into the library by way of replacement books should equal the issues that were taken out by the borrowers in the previous year. A comparison of the actual replacement rates in a library with those that should have occurred gives a good indication of the performance of the librarian in managing the library. Unfortunately, the financial pressures of recent years have meant that many librarians have not been performing as well as they might and this is especially true in those areas of popular, high-demand bookstock. Returning the library to a situation in which supply is more in tune with demand requires more drastic measures and these are discussed in the next chapter.

Chapter Five

Policy options

Within the overall constraint imposed by the book fund, the supply of books is something that is entirely under the control of the librarian. By injecting stock into or taking stock away from a library the librarian can control those books that are presented to the borrower on the shelves.˙Moreover, the librarian can change the way that books are presented. This can range from shelving books in a more attractive manner to a complete reclassification of the books and their presentation in a different and more attractive order. In presenting the choice to the borrower the librarian should bear in mind the demand expressed by the borrower for different types of books. By expressed demand we do not mean the occasional requests for material that are made to the librarian but demand as measured by the use of the stock as described in the previous chapter.

We are not suggesting that the librarian should concentrate on stocking the library with popular books to the exclusion of all others. Certainly the choice presented to the borrower in popular material shold be no less than the choice available in the less popular material. It should be stressed that whatever decisions are taken about stocking levels of different types of book these decisions must be based largely on value judgement by the librarian. No analytical technique is going to tell the librarian what the optimum stock levels should be and certainly we will not suggest in this book that libraries should cater only for popular demand. In practice the decisions that will be taken will be a compromise between the need to cater for mass demand on the one hand whilst maintaining a broadly-based and well-balanced stock on the other.

However the decision is taken on levels of stock it should

be expressed in the form of targets for shelf stock. The librarian should be aiming to present to the borrower groups of books on the shelves. Each group will have a target shelf stock which the librarian will try to maintain.

These targets provide a useful starting-point for policies directed at a particular library. In most cases a detailed review of a library will reveal that the actual situation in the library is very different from what it should be. Typically, popular groups of books will be under-represented with tired, worn-out stock whilst there are large numbers of relatively under-used books in the less popular groups sitting on shelves. If this is the situation then targets must be achieved before they can be maintained. This achievement of targets will involve wholesale stock injection and weeding of under-used books.

The aim of stock injection and weeding is to achieve the shelf stock targets that have already been set. If the shelf stock needs increasing then a stock injection is necessary. The size of this stock injection will be greater than the shortfall in shelf stock to allow for the fact that all stock spends some of its time out of the library on loan.

Stock injection and weeding policies are likely to affect the issues of the library over the longer term. Thus, as more stock becomes available in certain areas of the library the borrowing from those areas will increase and hence the issues will rise. Some of this increased borrowing will be drawn from outside the library as borrowers are encouraged to return by an enhanced range of choice. Some of the increase in issues will be taken from other areas of the library as existing borrowers transfer their allegiance from one area to another in response to the better choice available. The analysis of these shifting patterns of issues is complex and one that must be judged correctly if an overshoot of stock injection is to be avoided. The analysis needs a reliable data base on which to build and it is the building of this data base and its subsequent analysis that will be discussed in the following chapters.

The technique for assessing the correct levels of book withdrawal and replacement have already been discussed in the previous chapter. These levels can be calculated after the library has been restructured to ensure that supply targets are maintained. The replacement levels necessary to maintain supply targets are themselves targets for the librarian to adhere to. This introduces a new concept to the job of book acquisition. It is no longer sufficient to scan publishers' lists and select from the 'good' books. It is now necessary to ask further questions. First, the librarian must ask whether the book is needed to meet the targets, and second, whether it is a good buy in terms of the number of issues that it will achieve. Thus, stock acquisition becomes more complex, involving multiple trade-offs between on the one hand acquiring the sort of books the librarian would like to see in the library, and on the other hand filling the library with what might be regarded by some as 'trash' which is nevertheless what borrowers wish to read and will certainly earn its keep.

A recurring problem with libraries is the acquisition of the less popular books that are nevertheless necessary to achieve a balanced stock. In some very small libraries it has already been necessary to restrict the supply of books to the more popular material. Specialist books can be provided economically in small libraries by using rotating collections. The principle behind these collections is that individual libraries do not have the use of the books throughout their lifetime but enter into a 'timesharing' arrangement with other libraries whereby the collection stays in each library for a limited time only. Books for these rotating collections must be selected with care. Returning to the concepts of book circulation discussed in the previous chapter we can see that books that lose their circulation because of a decline in popularity over time are not suitable candidates for rotating collections. These books, once they are 'dead', are going to stay that way and no amount of movement between libraries is going to revive them.

In order to design rotating collections it is necessary to take a rather different view towards targets. The effect of a rotating collection is to make the books within it work harder. This means that they will tend to go out on loan rather than stay on the shelf. However, shelf stocks can remain relatively small because the choice being presented to the borrower is not from a wide stock of books on the shelves but a smaller stock that is constantly changing. In planning for a rotating collection, therefore, it is best not to target shelf stock but to target the annual issues that are to be achieved from the collection in each library it visits.

In summary, these opening chapters have described the public lending library and shown how the performance of it

and its librarian can be measured. This performance measurement adopts economic principles of measuring supply and
demand as well as the performance of the individual books
and the librarian in coping with these two factors. We have
then shown how this understanding can be built on to introduce policies into a library. These policies will be designed to
achieve and maintain targets set by the librarian. All this can
be achieved in practice as well as in theory by building on a
good data base. Subsequent chapters will describe how this
data base can be analysed to evaluate specific policies in
specific libraries.

Chapter Six

The systematic approach

The remainder of this book is concerned with applying the ideas outlined in the previous chapters as an aid to library management. The emphasis will be not on academic research but on developing a practical management tool that can be used by librarians to evaluate their policies. Throughout the succeeding chapters we will illustrate the methodology by worked examples. All these examples will assume, for simplicity, a single, self-contained library. Nevertheless the methodology if properly understood is equally applicable to groups of libraries or the whole library system. Indeed many of the benefits of this approach can only be enjoyed if there is some sort of system-wide management control and co-ordination.

The basis for the methodology is summed up in three words: survey, analysis and plan. In other words data are collected, analysed and then used to formulate and evaluate policy.

In most library systems and individual libraries there will already be a considerable amount of data that has been collected for annual returns, ad hoc enquiries and out of general interest. Most librarians will have some idea of the stock of books they keep in the library and how this stock is issued. This preliminary assessment of a library is discussed in chapter 7. However, although a general picture is available, rarely will it extend to detailed breakdowns by groups of books.

A more detailed picture can only be obtained by carrying out some sort of survey. The main purpose of such a survey will be to assemble data on the behaviour of groups of books within the library. A number of data sources are possible.

There is the whole stock of books as listed in the catalogue. There is the shelf stock. There are returned books and there are withdrawn books. Each of these has its story to tell and the technique of extracting data from them is discussed in chapter 8.

When the data have been obtained from a survey they must be processed to yield useful and reliable information. The techniques for producing some preliminary tabulations are discussed in chapter 9. These tabulations will include details, by category of book, of stock, issues, average age and average loan period.

Once a data base has been established it can be expanded to incorporate other information. This expansion of data requires a number of logical relationships, some of which have been derived and explained in previous chapters. By the end of chapter 10 a full data matrix has been derived containing a summary of all the information about a library that is necessary for management purposes.

However the raw data in this matrix are of little value on their own. Before they can be used as an aid to management decisions they must be interpreted. They must be checked for consistency and logicality. The underlying assumptions must be scrutinized carefully and amended if necessary. Measures of demand, supply, performance and policy can then be extracted from the matrix and interpreted to point to certain policy directions. This interpretation is discussed in chapter 11.

The interpreted data can be used to formulate and evaluate policy. This stage will use well-tried principles of engineering design — draw it first and then design it. In other words, different policies are drawn up, tested using the information from the data matrix and then reformulated. Amongst the policy options that are discussed in chapter 12, 13 and 14 are stock injection, withdrawal and replacement of stock, and stock rotation between libraries.

By this stage we will have a powerful tool that can be used for planning and managing library systems. However, this process of planning and management is not a unique exercise in time but one that must be kept up to date. Moreover, the information used, in some cases to trigger new policies, must also be updated. This process of monitoring is discussed in chapter 15.

All this activity must be reflected in the organizational structure of public library departments. Some of the organizational implications of systematic bookstock management are discussed in chapter 16.

Finally, because the methods discussed in chapters 7 to 15 are many and complex, they will be summarized in the form of a 'cookbook' in chapter 17. This is intended as an aid to application for those who understand the methods. It is no substitute for the chapters previous to it in gaining essential understanding.

Chapter Seven

Preliminary assessment

In any library there will be a considerable amount of information already to hand. As a prelude to any data collection exercise it is important to carry out a preliminary assessment of the library to find out just how much information there is. In addition it will be necessary to understand fully the procedures adopted in the library. This enquiry will be conducted under four main headings. First, there is the bookstock itself, its size, arrangement, cataloguing, etc. Second, there are the loans from the library and the issuing system, the number of issues per year, the recording of issues, and the number of books on loan at any time. Third, there are the circulation characteristics of individual books or groups of books within the library. Much of this information and indeed most of what follows in this book will depend on there being date-stamp labels in all books as a record of past issues. We would also like to know the life of books and which books are popular. Fourth, there are the current policies adopted by the librarian. These will include withdrawal policies, replacement policies, stock refurbishment policies, etc.

Bookstock
The stock of a library is probably its greatest and most obvious asset. Many libraries will still have a catalogue which purports to record all items of bookstock currently kept by the library. Unless a lot of work is put into catalogues they tend to become out-of-date and unreliable as sources of information. Even if new books are meticulously recorded and withdrawals from stock deleted from the catalogue, there will still be unrecorded losses and thefts from the library. This means that the catalogue usually represents an

over-estimate of the number of books contained in a library. Occasionally a stock-taking will be carried out which will update the catalogue. However, such stock-taking exercises are time-consuming operations and for this reason rarely carried out nowadays. Where counts have been carried out to reconcile the stock to the catalogue, discrepancies of 15 to 20 per cent have been found. Some librarians try to maintain a record of the total amount of stock by continually updating the most recent stock-taking figure with withdrawals and replacements. This method too suffers from the defect that it is difficult to keep track of lost books.

The shelf stock in the library will be obvious and visible. However, this represents only a proportion of the total stock, the remainder being out on loan. In individual groups of books, for example popular fiction, the proportion out on loan may be as high as 80 or 90 per cent. Thus, the shelf stock in these groups represents a small and unrepresentative sample of the whole stock. Nevertheless, it is useful to carry out a count of the shelf stock as a prelude to data collection.

The stock on loan is not as visible as the stock on the shelf but it can be seen as it passes through the library in the form of issues and returns. There are other groups of books in the library in addition to shelf stock and stock on loan. Some libraries maintain a reserve stock of books. If this is so, it is probably best to treat this stock apart from the main stock and to examine borrowing from reserve separately.

Some libraries do not immediately throw away the books that they withdraw from the shelves. An accumulation of withdrawn books can form a useful data resource.

The arrangement of stock on shelves has important repercussions for any subsequent analysis work. There are the Dewey diehards and the categorization enthusiasts among librarians. It is not the purpose of this book to enter this debate but merely to take notice of whatever exists and work within it.

Issues

All lending libraries issue books. Often daily counts are maintained of the number of issues. These counts are usually subdivided into major book grouping (eg fiction, non-fiction, junior, etc).

There are three main types of issuing systems in use.

There is the traditional Browne system in which the ticket from a book is put together with the borrower's ticket and they are stored in groups by date of issue. This system is effective but labour-intensive. To provide a less labour-intensive system some libraries have adopted a token system. With this system borrowers are issued with a number of plastic tokens which they can exchange for a book. Some libraries use a combination of a Browne system and a token system, for example by using one for non-fiction issues and the other for fiction issues. Both these manual systems are giving way to computerized issuing systems.

With all types of issuing systems it is possible to make an estimate of the number of books on loan at any time. However, the accuracy of the estimate will vary. With a token system especially the estimate may be highly unreliable because it will include those books that have been issued but will never return. On the other hand, computerized systems can supply very precise information.

Circulation characteristics
Few librarians will have much idea of the circulation characteristics of individual books. True, there will be much subjective and anecdotal evidence as librarians observe books disappearing from certain shelves or passing quickly and in great numbers across the issuing counters. However, information is available in the form of date stamps inside the books. Much of what will be said in succeeding chapters will depend on this information being available.

Library policies
As well as the evidence of the date stamp there will be other factors that affect book circulation. The maximum loan period is the most important of these but it is also interesting to know the maximum number of books that a borrower can withdraw at any time.

It is also important to establish the organization and policy context in which the library operates. The nature of the management structure will have an important relationship to subsequent policy analysis. The book fund available to the library should be noted both for the current year and for previous years. All information on the number and type of books acquired for the library should be assembled.

Withdrawal policy should be noted and any records of with-drawal should be retained. Stock circulating between libraries will behave differently from stock staying in one library, so if there is a policy of bookstock rotation it should be under-stood and its parameters recorded. Any changes in policy should be noted.

Much of this information may be obvious at the outset but it is worth drawing it all together in a consistent form before any further survey or analysis takes place.

Summary

In summary, this chapter has concluded that it will be poss-ible in most libraries to establish the stock of books, split by the stock on shelf and that on loan, and the annual issues from the stock. It will also be possible to get some insight into current and past management policies in the library. Most of the available data will be in aggregate form. There will be little or no information on individual groups of books within the library. To obtain this information it will be necessary to conduct and analyse a survey. It is these procedures that are discussed in the following chapters.

Chapter Eight

Survey

Although we may find a lot of data in the records of the library we are studying it is likely that we will not find sufficient to make the sort of policy decisions that are necessary. In particular, information about the different categories of books is missing. To supplement the data found in the library we must carry out some sort of survey.

The purpose of the survey is to obtain information that is not already obtainable from library records. In particular we would like to know more about how individual books and categories of books behave. Thus the survey will be designed to obtain information about the amount of stock in a number of categories, the rate of issues from each category, the age of the stock in each category and loan periods. In addition to this we have already discussed the importance of the circulation characteristics of individual books and we would like to collect data that can be used to give us insight into this.

The purpose of this book is to discuss bookstock and how it behaves in a public library. However, this is only a means to the end of providing a service to the borrower. We are using survey techniques to find out how books behave but we could equally well use a survey to find out how borrowers behave and what their motivations are. Borrower surveys will be touched upon in this chapter.

Before we carry out a survey we have to decide what we are surveying. Are we surveying books or people? Which books are we trying to survey? Is it those books in the library now? Is it those books that have been withdrawn from the library or is it new acquisitions? Which people are we trying to survey? Are we surveying registered users of the library or are we surveying those people who actually visit the library and borrow books?

Sampling

Most surveys that are carried out are based on the theory of sampling. That is, one does not have to measure everyone and everything in order to get a fairly good picture of what is happening. Provided we pick a representative subset of the things we are trying to survey we can build up quite a reliable picture. Moreover, this subset or sample, if properly chosen, need not be very large.

There are two main criteria for choosing a sample. It must be unbiased and it must be easily accessible. An unbiased sample is one that is truly representative of the population being surveyed. Items must be selected for the sample in as random a manner as possible from a sample frame that contains all the group that is of interest. It is also no good picking a sampling technique that is impossible to implement. For instance, it would be inefficient to pick a borrower out of a list of registered library users and then have to track that person down.

The group from which we select our sample is called the sample frame. The most obvious sample frame is the total stock of books in the library as recorded in the catalogue. We could draw from the catalogue a random list of books and then attempt to find them and record data from them. Although this sampling method gives an unbiased sample it is hardly an accessible one. The same comments apply to using the list of registered borrowers as the sampling frame for a survey of people using the library.

A more accessible sample frame is represented by the books on the shelf. However, although accessible this sample frame is unfortunately biased. Books on the shelf tend to be those that people do not borrow and therefore they will not give a representative picture of the borrowing behaviour of the users of the library. The bias can be redressed by also surveying books out on loan. It is not practicable to try to find these books on loan by visiting borrowers in their homes but they can be captured when they are taken out or returned. It is probably easier to survey books that are being returned and to survey them after they have been discharged. If, however, we wish to combine this survey of returned books with a survey of borrowers, then it may be necessary to interview the borrowers and inspect their books before they are actually discharged.

Another possible sample frame consists of withdrawn books. This is an attractive source of data as it is highly accessible. Moreover, it is the only accurate way of getting quickly a precise picture of the way books are used over their lifetimes. However, this source suffers from a number of disadvantages. First, there may not be sufficient of these books available to give a large enough sample. Second, the information obtained from this source will be historical and cannot be used to determine how current books are being used.

For the purpose of further discussion we will assume that we are going to carry out a survey of books on the shelf and returned books. This survey of current bookstock may be supplemented by a survey of withdrawn stock and by a survey of borrowers' behaviour and attitudes.

Once the sample frame has been established, a technique must be chosen to pick an unbiased sample from the sample frame. Two techniques will be discussed here: a quota sample and a sample arrived at by regular selection.

A quota sample is used for a survey of returned books, for example. The technique is simple. We decide how big a sample we require and then we continue surveying books until the sample size is reached.

Regular selection is used for shelf stock, for example. In this case we make some estimate of the total shelf stock and decide what size sample we require. We then divide one by the other to get a sampling rate. Let us suppose this is 1 in 10. We generate a random number between 1 and 10, say 6. We then start at some convenient point in the library. We find the sixth book along, survey it, replace it and then count to the tenth book from this position. We continue surveying each tenth book until we have covered the library.

The reason for carrying out a sample rather than a full survey is that it requires less effort for an acceptably good result. However, the sample size must be chosen carefully to ensure that the results of the survey are reliable. Note that it is the size of the sample that is important, not the sample rate. We can illustrate this point with an example.

Let us suppose we have decided to mount a survey of returned books. Let us further suppose that the only information we are interested in is the distribution of those books by category. Now if we start the survey and tabulate the results as we go, initially, with data from only a few books, we will find that distribution of books by category will change as new items of data are added from the survey. Eventually, however, the result becomes stable and is unaffected by further additions. The point at which the result becomes stable is the sample size that we are trying to estimate. This sample size will not depend on the total number of books being returned but it will depend on the number of categories selected.

Without going into mathematical detail — consult a statistical textbook* if you are interested — it is possible to establish some coarse rules of thumb on an acceptable sample size. It is worth remembering that data from library books are easy to obtain and if we find later in the process that we have got an inadequate sample we can always go back for more.

For the time being we will aim to split our bookstock into about forty categories and to survey about fifty books in each category. Note that the total sample size will be determined by the smallest category. The minimum total sample size will be achieved when categories are selected so that there is an equal number of books in each. One of the practical difficulties of determining sample size is that until we have carried out the survey we will not have reliable estimates of the factors which influence sample size. Nevertheless, intelligent guesses can be made and if those prove wrong, then either adjustments can be made as discussed in the next chapter or, as stated above, we can go back for more data.

Let us look at an example of selecting sample size. We wish to carry out a survey of shelf stock and returned books in a library containing a total of 20,000 books. Half of these books are on the shelf and the other half on loan. We have decided to split the books into forty categories. Assuming for the moment that the number of books in each category is approximately the same, it looks as though we require a sample of 2,000 books. 1,000 books have to be drawn from the shelf stock, so we take a 1 in 10 regular selection as described above and a quota of 1,000 returned books will be surveyed.

We have already referred to book categories and one

* eg Yeomans, K A *Statistics for the social scientist* 2 vols (Penguin, 1970) or Moroney, M J *Facts from figures* (Penguin, 1969).

criterion for their designation, namely that the number of
books in each category is about the same. In selecting suitable
categories for analysis there are two further conflicting
criteria. On the one hand, it is important to get groups of
books that are meaningful to the librarian (and the borrower).
In a categorized library, for example, there will be a temp-
tation to use the categories already designated. However, at
the end of the analysis we are going to be making assumptions
that individual books in a category behave very much like
each other. Thus, we have the need for homogeneity conflicting with the need for comprehensibility. Inevitably this
conflict will have to be resolved in a pragmatic way. One
possibility is to use the librarian's categories as a basis but to
split individual categories to reflect the mix of different
types of books within the category. For example, it may be
useful to split a fiction category into paperback and hardback
groups, each of which has significantly different circulation
characteristics.

The questionnaire

For the information to be recorded systematically it will be
necessary to design some sort of form or questionnaire. In
doing this it must be remembered that the person carrying
out the survey may not be the survey designer. All definitions
must, therefore, be quite explicit and it should be possible to
fill in the survey form without any prior interpretation by
the surveyor.

Below is illustrated an actual survey form used for a survey
of shelf stock and returned books.

BOOKSTOCK SURVEY

Library . . . .   Date . . . .   Type . . . .

Name of Surveyor . . . .

No	Dewey No	Cat	Format	Issues/yr	Date of addition	Date due back

At the top of each sheet there is some heading information. The name of the survey assistant should be recorded so that everyone knows whom to blame. The date of the survey may also be necessary for processing the data and should be recorded. If the survey is being carried out at more than one library, then the library name should go on the heading. The type of survey, that is, shelf stock, returned books, withdrawn books, should also be recorded and it may also be useful to record on the heading the major groups of books that are being surveyed (eg fiction or non-fiction).

In the body of the survey form there will be a number of rows, each row representing a single book. Information for each book will be filled in under column headings. Each book surveyed should be given a consecutive sequence number. This is recorded in the first column. This information is necessary so that if problems arise during the analysis we can link up or 'reconcile' survey data with records used for analysis.

In the next columns there will be a description of the book. There are two choices here. We can draw up a precise classification of books that can be understood by the survey assistant who assigns each book to its pre-determined category. This is all very well provided we do not wish to modify the classification system during the analysis. There is nothing more frustrating than deciding that we would like information on, for example, paperbacks, only to find that there is no way of identifying the paperbacks in the sample. The other alternative is to record all possible information describing the book even down to title and author. Certainly this is playing it safe but the penalty may be excessive time spent carrying out the survey. In practice a compromise will be struck with some redundant classification data being collected but stopping short of recording full bibliographic details of each book surveyed.

In the example shown we have recorded the category of the book because it was a categorized library that was being surveyed, the Dewey number of the book in the case of non-fiction, the format of the book (ie paperback, hardback, large print, etc). We could also have used codes to describe the level of treatment, condition of book, etc.

The date stamps of all the books will be examined to find out the pattern of issues. At the very least the number of issues in the last twelve months should be recorded. In the case of withdrawn books especially, we may also wish to record the number of issues on a year-by-year basis throughout the life of the book to date. Obtaining such information from a book will depend on the date-stamp labels having been preserved. The survey assistant should be provided with a kettle as standard equipment.

The age of the book, that is, the length of time it has been in the library, can be inferred from the date on which the book was acquired. If this information is recorded in the book then it should be noted on the survey form. Failing this, the date of the first issue should be used as a proxy.

For returned books we would also like to know the amount of time they have been out on loan. This information can be inferred from the date of the last date stamp which should be recorded.

For withdrawn books it may also be useful to record the reason for withdrawal. Was it because the book was physically worn out, out of date, no longer circulating, etc? Codes will be assigned to these various reasons to make the job of survey easier.

Processing the results
When the survey has been carried out, the sheets of paper must be processed in some way to make the data available for analysis. There is really no substitute for a desk-top microcomputer as an aid to survey analysis and we will assume that one can be made available. Nowadays it is not necessary to be a computer expert to use these machines. In addition to readily available, proprietary survey-analysis packages, there is also available general-purpose data-analysis software that goes under the generic term of 'spreadsheet analysis' programs'. Some of these are exceedingly good and very easy to use. They are sufficiently flexible to perform all the analysis that we are likely to wish to perform on the data. All data analysis used in the rest of this book by way of illustration has been done with such a program.

The first task to be performed on the survey data is to enter it into the computer so that it can be stored in some machine-readable form (eg on a floppy disk). As a prelude to this process it may be necessary to go through the survey sheets and check the information. In some cases it may also be necessary to use codes for information which the surveyor has entered in full. There is little point in entering the title of a book into a computer as all the machine will be able to do with it is to print it out again. Category codes, Dewey numbers, format codes, etc are all acceptable and can be analysed by computers quite easily.

Once we have got the informâtion in machine-readable form, then we can use the computer to do some initial processing. It is usually convenient to combine this stage with a validation process. The purpose of the initial processing will be to convert a file of survey records into a file of records that contain data that are more directly analysable. For example, it will be necessary to convert the date on the last date stamp to a loan period. To do this the computer will have been set up with a simple formula that says that

Loan period = The maximum loan period less the interval between survey date and date of last stamp in days

Similar formulae will be used to convert the date of acquisition into the age of the book. At this stage, if we have not already done so, the computer will assign each record to a category for analysis purposes. A typical format for the output file is given below:

Field	Contents
1	Survey type
2	Sequence number
3	Category
4	Age
5	Number of issues last year
6	Loan period

Whilst carrying out these transformations on the data it will also be necessary to check each field. This is to guard against errors both in the survey and the coding processes. These checks will be carried out by the computer by using acceptable ranges for each data field. For example, to guard against the surveyor having recorded the wrong year on the last date stamp it will be necessary to impose a maximum and a minimum on the loan period (say 150 days and 0 days). Any records with data outside this range will be identified or 'flagged' for further examination. In many cases it will be

Table 1 Summary of survey information

Category	Shelf books	Return books	Total books
1 Bus St	14	9	23
2 Relig	17	14	31
3 Homes	26	20	46
4 Food	11	10	21
5 Medic	6	7	13
6 Garden	16	10	26
7 Transp	17	19	36
8 Railway	6	11	17
9 Soc Sc	33	18	51
10 Science	9	0	9
11 Country	24	14	38
12 Animals	11	13	24
13 Sport	30	19	49
14 Art	39	11	50
15 Music	15	7	22
16 Photo	5	7	12
17 Biog	35	42	77
18 Lit	24	12	36
19 Milit	21	20	41
20 Geog	58	24	82
21 Hist	38	27	65
22 Misc	21	5	26
Sub total	476	319	795
23 Gen Fic	159	230	389
24 Mystery	21	129	150
25 Romance	8	54	62
26 Western	3	12	15
27 Sci Fi	9	8	17
28 Hist	39	70	109
29 Large P	20	113	133
30 Short S	10	3	13
31 Yng Ad	5	8	13
32 Pap Bk	51	330	381
Sub total	325	957	1282
Grand total	801	1276	2077

possible, by referring back to the original survey form (and this is where the sequence number proves its worth), to find out what the data should have been and to correct or convert them. However, we must never invent data and should it be impossible to put in an acceptable value we must have some convention for identifying the elements of the record that are not to be used for the purposes of analysis. Thus, if we are unable to determine the age of a particular book because the required information was either not collected or collected inaccurately, then we must identify or flag that record. Then when calculating the average age of the books in a category the flagged record will not be used although other information about that particular book may be used for other purposes.

Finally, the survey process will be rounded off by producing some summary tables just to show what information has been collected. At this stage we may wish to know simply how many books were surveyed in each category in each type of survey — shelf stock, returned books, withdrawn books. Table 1 is an example of such a table. In the next chapter we will deal with ways of processing the survey information further to obtain more detailed information by category.

Chapter Nine

Assembling the information

The end result of the survey process is a number of records, one for each book that was surveyed. These raw data are of little value for analysis purposes and must be transformed into summaries which present data for individual categories.

In the course of this process we must overcome two problems. First the data we have obtained from the surveys may not tie up with the data already obtained by inspection of library records. It will therefore be necessary to make some form of judgement as to which is the correct data and to adjust accordingly. Second, if we have collected from more than one source, eg stock on shelf and returned books, then data from the two sources must be combined together in some way so as to give a true and unbiased picture of the whole library.

To be more specific we wish to take data from the surveys and make estimates of the amount of stock in each category so that the total stock of the library found by adding up the estimates for the various categories tallies with the information that we already have from library records. We will then wish to find the annual issues for each category and the average age of books from each category. Note that all this information is obtained from the surveys of shelf stock and returned books. Other surveys, of withdrawn books or interviews of borrowers, for example, have their place but are not discussed in this chapter.

The survey of shelf stock presents no problem of inter-pretation. We know the sample rate used and we can use this sample rate in reverse to make estimates of shelf stock by category. Thus, if we took a 1 in 10 sample and surveyed 35 books on the shelf in one category, then our estimate of the actual number of books on the shelf in that category is 350 (ie 10 × 35).

The survey of returned books and hence books on loan presents a rather more difficult problem. In this case we did not take a uniform sample rate but a quota. Before we can gross up or 'factor up' the results of the survey we need to know what this quota was as a percentage of total books on loan. It may be that we have a reliable estimate of this from counting the issue tickets in a Browne issuing system or from a printout from a computerized issuing system. However, this information may be unreliable and if a token issuing system is used will certainly be so. It may be necessary to make an independent estimate of the total number of books out on loan at the time the survey took place.

Fortunately we can calculate the number of books on loan if we know the total annual issues and the average loan period. There is a formula that states:

$$\text{Books on loan} = \frac{\text{Annual issues} \times \text{Average loan period}}{365}$$

This formula was derived in an earlier chapter. Since we have a reliable esimate of the annual issues in the library we can make an estimate of the books on loan, provided we know the average loan period.

Our first task, therefore, is to calculate the average loan period from the data. This information can be derived from the survey of returned books. Moreover, it is independent of the sample rate that we took because we can make the assumption that the average loan period of our sample of returned books is the same as the average loan period of all books. Briefly, then, we take our survey information, add up all the valid loan periods from the survey and divide by the number of valid records. It may be that the annual issues are broken down by major groupings of books such as fiction and non-fiction. If this is the case we can also make an estimate of the books on loan in these groupings, provided we obtain a corresponding average loan period. This too can be extracted from the survey by splitting the data into two or more groups and carrying out the analysis described above on each group. Note that we carry out the analysis on valid records, that is, records for which we have valid loan period information. As described in the previous chapter there may

be some records for which no valid information is available
and these should be ignored in this analysis.

Once we have made our estimate of total books on loan
we can work out a sampling factor for the returned books
survey. This sampling factor is found by using the following
formula:

$$\text{Sampling factor} = \frac{\text{Total books on loan}}{\text{Number of returned books surveyed}}$$

Note that if the data are available it is worth finding separate
sampling factors for both fiction and non-fiction groupings.
These will be different even when both books were picked up
indiscriminately in the same quota because typically loan
periods will differ between the two groups.

The whole of this process can be illustrated with an
example.

Non fiction

Issues per year	=	62,362
Average loan period	=	20·21 days
Books on loan	=	$\dfrac{62,362 \times 20·21}{365}$
	=	3,453
Number of returned books surveyed	=	319
Sample factor	=	$\dfrac{3,453}{319}$
	=	10·82

In other words, we sampled one book in every 10·82 books
on loan.

In summary we have two sets of sampling factors, one for
each survey. These differential sampling factors enable us to
compensate for the fact that we may have used a different
sample rate in each survey and they can be used to produce
unbiased estimates of aggregate data. Incidentally, this ability
to sort out the survey once it is completed by using differential sampling factors enables us to supplement our
original survey data with more selective additions. For
example, we may find that our original sample rate gave us
a less than adequate sample of the shelf stock in one of the
categories. We could return to the shelves in this particular
category and carry out a new survey with a higher sampling
rate which could then be used to replace the original data

in this category. The new data could be added to the existing returned books data using the sampling factor techniques described above. The sampling factors can now be used with the data to produce for each category information about such parameters as total stock, annual issues and average age of the stock.

The amount of stock in each category can be obtained by using the tabulation we obtained at the end of the survey process which shows the number of books surveyed in each category broken down by type of survey.

To obtain an estimate of total stock in each category we apply the appropriate sample factors to the information from each survey and add the results together. So, for example:

Category 4 — Food

Number of books from shelf	=	11
Number of returned books surveyed	=	10
Sampling factor for shelf stock	=	10
Sampling factor for returned books	=	10·82
Total stock	=	(11 × 10) + (10 × 10·82)
	=	218

The same process can be applied in order to calculate the annual issues by category. We can use the count of the issues in the last twelve months from each book and again apply sample factors to this information. Note that there may not be information on issues for each book surveyed if, for example, date labels have been defaced or removed. If this is the case it may be necessary to adjust our sample factors for each survey type before applying them. Remember the formula for sampling factors:

$$\text{Sample factor} = \frac{\text{Number of valid records from survey}}{\text{Total size of group surveyed}}$$

The estimate for annual issues by category can then be summed for all categories and compared with the independent estimate obtained by the librarian or from library records. There is likely to be some small discrepancy because our estimate does not take into account issues contributed by books that are subsequently withdrawn. Nevertheless, there should be a good correspondence between the two figures and this should encourage us to accept the data we have

Table 2 Initial information

Category	Stock	Is/yr	Age
1 Bus St	237	2020	2·09
2 Relig	321	2805	5·52
3 Homes	476	4160	3·36
4 Food	218	2310	3·08
5 Medic	136	1193	5·47
6 Garden	268	2436	5·95
7 Transp	376	3465	3·98
8 Railway	179	2089	4·68
9 Soc Sc	525	3480	4·05
10 Science	90	400	3·59
11 Country	391	4381	4·89
12 Animals	251	2467	4·71
13 Sport	506	4098	4·06
14 Art	509	2764	4·86
15 Music	226	1870	3·55
16 Photo	126	1425	2·37
17 Biog	804	8842	7·49
18 Lit	370	2493	5·42
19 Milit	426	4426	5·15
20 Geog	840	5714	6·95
21 Hist	672	5233	6·19
22 Misc	264	1241	4·41
Sub total	8211	69312	5·09
23 Gen Fic	3391	38976	5·71
24 Mystery	1220	22508	3·86
25 Romance	503	9105	2·98
26 Western	124	1231	3·31
27 Sci Fi	153	1397	5·28
28 Hist	938	11262	4·53
29 Large P	1085	17051	2·75
30 Short S	123	819	5·41
31 Yng Ad	113	710	3·71
32 Pap Bk	3094	54403	1·33
Sub total	10744	157462	3·65
Grand total	18955	226774	4·27

obtained and proceed with the analysis. If there is a poor correspondence then the likeliest explanation is an arithmetical error in calculating sample factors which should be corrected before proceeding.

The average age of the stock by category can now be found. The process is one that is similar to the two preceding. In this case the age of the book from the survey information is multiplied by the appropriate sample factor and cumulated for each category. These cumulative ages are then divided by the total stock in each category to get an average age. Remember that if there are bad data it will be necessary to find new sample factors and to estimate the total stock in each category for which valid data are available.

These three items of data can now be tabulated in a form as shown in Table 2. It will be these items of data that are used as a basis for subsequent analysis.

Before we move on to this analysis let us go back to the measurement of average loan periods. We saw earlier how average loan periods could be calculated for the whole stock and for major groupings. This methodology could also be applied to individual small groups. Unfortunately this calculation depends only on data from the returned books survey. It may be that in some categories we will have a very small or non-existent sample. We cannot produce answers from no data and the answer we get from small samples may be inaccurate. For subsequent analysis, therefore, we will use average loan periods for the major groups (fiction and non-fiction) and not for individual categories. Nevertheless, it is interesting to get accurate information on loan period by category as there tends to be systematic and significant variation. To do this it may be necessary to conduct a special survey at a later date or, better still, to make use of a computerized issuing system.

With data on loan periods it is also possible to investigate patterns. Figure 5 reproduces two graphs showing the frequency distribution of fiction and non-fiction loan periods in a library where the maximum loan period was 3 weeks. It is interesting to note the peaks that occur at 7, 14 and 21 days, no doubt due to borrowers acquiring the library habit. It is also interesting to note the tail on the distribution after the 3 weeks showing the incidence of overdue books.

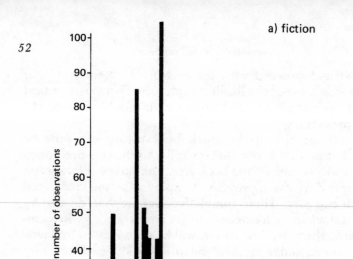

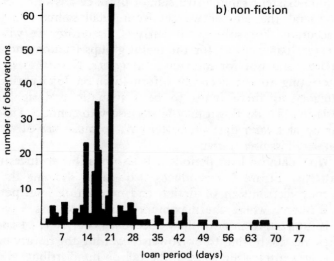

Figure 5 Frequency distributions of loan period drawn from survey

Chapter Ten

Analysis

In the last chapter we saw how we could assemble some basic information about the bookstock and how we could break down this information into the various categories. This chapter will show us how we can squeeze even more information from our basic survey data by using some simple logical relationships.

For example, we can get useful measures of performance for the stock as a whole by looking at the proportions on loan and on the shelf in the different categories.

The basic building-blocks of any library are the books and we can learn a lot about these by studying their circulation characteristics. Thus, the number of issues a book achieves each year is a useful measure of its performance. The variation in the issues on a year-by-year basis and the total issues that a book will achieve over its lifetime are both useful pointers to the contribution a book will make to the library.

Finally, and crucially, we can calculate the replacement and withdrawal rates that are necessary to sustain stock and issues at their current level.

Throughout this chapter we will be building up a data matrix in which is summarized all the information about books in each category. A blank matrix is illustrated in Table 3.

Each row of the matrix represents one of our categories. For ease of reference each category, in addition to a reference number, is given a mnemonic. It will be useful to summarize results by fiction or non-fiction grouping. A line for sub total (or group averages) is provided in the table for this purpose.

Each column of the matrix represents an item of data.

Table 3 Blank data matrix

Category	Stock	Is/yr	Age	Bk ln	Bk sh	Pr ln	I/Y/B	Life	Tot Is	Rep R
1 Bus St										
2 Relig										
3 Homes										
4 Food										
5 Medic										
6 Garden										
7 Transp										
8 Railway										
9 Soc Sc										
10 Science										
11 Country										
12 Animals										
13 Sport										
14 Art										
15 Music										
16 Photo										
17 Biog										
18 Lit										
19 Milit										
20 Geog										
21 Hist										
22 Misc										
Sub total										

23	Gen Fic
24	Mystery
25	Romance
26	Western
27	Sci Fi
28	Hist
29	Large P
30	Short S
31	Yng Ad
32	Pap Bk

Sub total

Grand total

Key

Is/yr	=	Issues per year
Bk ln	=	Books on loan
Bk sh	=	Books on shelf
Pr ln	=	Proportion on loan
I/Y/B	=	Issues per year per book
Tot Is	=	Total issues
Rep R	=	Replacement rate

Table 4 Data matrix with initial information

Category	Stock	Is/yr	Age	Bk ln	Bk sh	Pr ln	I/Y/B	Life	Tot Is	Rep R
1 Bus St	237	2020	2·09							
2 Relig	321	2805	5·52							
3 Homes	476	4160	3·36							
4 Food	218	2310	3·08							
5 Medic	136	1193	5·47							
6 Garden	268	2436	5·95							
7 Transp	376	2465	3·98							
8 Railway	179	2089	4·68							
9 Soc Sc	525	3480	4·05							
10 Science	90	400	3·59							
11 Country	391	4381	4·89							
12 Animals	251	2467	4·71							
13 Sport	506	4098	4·06							
14 Art	509	2764	4·86							
15 Music	226	1870	3·55							
16 Photo	126	1425	2·37							
17 Biog	804	8842	7·49							
18 Lit	370	2493	5·42							
19 Milit	426	4426	5·15							
20 Geog	840	5714	6·95							
21 Hist	672	5233	6·19							
22 Misc	264	1241	4·41							
Sub total	8211	69312	5·09							

23	Gen Fic	3391	38976	5·71
24	Mystery	1220	22508	3·86
25	Romance	503	9105	2·98
26	Western	124	1231	3·31
27	Sci Fi	153	1397	5·28
28	Hist	938	11262	4·53
29	Large P	1085	17051	2·75
30	Short S	123	819	5·41
31	Yng Ad	113	710	3·71
32	Pap Bk	3094	54403	1·33
	Sub total	10744	157462	3·65
	Grand total	18955	226774	4·27

The first three items of data — stock, issues per year and average age of the stock — have been processed using techniques described in the previous chapter. We can now reproduce our data matrix with this information filled in (Table 4).

In the remainder of this chapter we will build up the rest of the matrix one column at a time. To illustrate the techniques involved we will take one row of the matrix — category 4, Food — and fill in the figures.

Books on loan

It may be that we have already done a direct count of the number of books on loan by category. This can be done either by counting the tickets in a Browne issuing system, a tedious process, or more likely as a by-product of a computerized issuing system. If this is the case, then we can fill this information in straight away.

In many cases the only way to this information is by a sample survey of shelf stock and returned books. If this is the case, then there are a number of ways of arriving at the number of books on loan by category.

Assume for a moment that we have carried out a survey of returned books and then worked out the sample factors as described in the previous chapter. This information can be used to find the number of books on loan in each category by multiplying the number of books in each category that were surveyed by the appropriate sampling factor. The snag with this method is that it is quite conceivable that for small categories of under-used books we may not have picked up any book in our survey of returned books. Thus our estimate of the number of books on loan in these categories would be zero. This is despite the evidence of the date stamp of those books that were surveyed from the shelf which suggests that the books are loaned.

To overcome this problem we can calculate the number of books on loan by using the issues per year from each category and the average loan period for each category. We do this by using the formula discussed in the previous chapter. That is:

$$\text{Books on loan} = \frac{\text{Issues per year} \times \text{Average loan period}}{365}$$

However, if we have to rely on a survey of returned books to estimate average loan periods by category then we are no better off than we were in using the first method. This method is of use if we have information on loan periods by category derived independently of survey from a computerized issuing system, for example.

If we have only a survey of returned books and shelf stock to use, then we must fall back on the third method. This consists of using the formula given above but substituting in it the loan period of the group of books (fiction or non-fiction) in which the category is contained. The answer obtained by using this method will be sufficiently reliable to be acceptable.

To illustrate this let us take our example and do the calculation.

Category 4 — Food

Issues per year	=	2310
Average loan period for non-fiction	=	20·21 days
Number of books on loan	=	$\dfrac{2310 \times 20\cdot21}{365}$
	=	128

Stock on shelf

If we have carried out a survey of the shelf stock we may have a direct estimate of the number of books on the shelf in each category. However, if we add this to the number of books on loan that we have just derived we will arrive at a figure for the total stock in each category that is not consistent with the figure in column one of the table. We therefore have a choice. On the one hand we can accept the figure for total stock and derive the number of books on the shelf or we can accept the figure for shelf stock and revise the total stock figure. For the larger categories there will not be a significant difference between the methods. For smaller categories the differences will not significantly affect the overall picture. On balance it is probably better to accept the estimate of the total stock in each category and work from it.

Stock on shelf can therefore be obtained using the simple formula:

Stock on shelf = Total stock − Stock on loan

Illustrating this we can proceed with our example:

Category 4 — Food

Stock	=	218
Number of books on loan	=	128
Stock on shelf	=	218 − 128
	=	90

Proportion on loan

The proportion of the stock on loan is an important measure of the demand for books in the category. It will be used in later chapters. It can be derived from the total stock and the stock on loan by the simple formula:

$$\text{Proportion of stock on loan} = \frac{\text{Stock on loan}}{\text{Total stock}}$$

It is worth referring back to chapter 3 in which the concept of probabilities was discussed. The proportion of the stock on loan is equivalent to the proportion of time that an average book in the category is on loan, which in turn is equivalent to the probability that the average book will be on loan.

Again, illustrating this measure with our example we have:

Stock on loan	=	128
Total stock	=	218
Proportion of stock on loan	=	0·587

That is, 58·7 per cent of the stock is on loan. An average book in this category spends 58·7 per cent of its time (ie 214 days a year) on loan and there is a 58·7 per cent probability that the average book will be on loan at any time.

Circulation characteristics

In earlier chapters we discussed the circulation curve of an individual book. This circulation curve can be summarized in the form of three parameters: the life of the book in years; the total issues that a book achieves in its lifetime; and the average issues that a book achieves each year of its life. These three measures can be averaged for all books in a category and give us useful insight into the performance of a typical book in different categories.

There are two ways in which these parameters can be derived from data. The first and most obvious way is to analyse the circulation of individual withdrawn books. The second way involves applying some approximations to the data we have already derived for the category.

If we have collected some circulation history from a number of books in a survey of withdrawn books we can tabulate the data in a form as shown in Table 5.

Table 5 Withdrawn books data

Year	1	2	3	4	5	6	7	8	9	10	Mean
1	16	18	2	2	10	12	16	3	2	14	9·5
2	17	17	4	2	3	9	7	3	6	14	8·2
3	17	17	0	0	5	10	3	2	3	5	6·2
4	12		3	1	4	4	8	2	4	6	4·4
5	14		0	2	0	3	2	6	9		3·6
6	8		0	1	3	6	4	3	5		3·0
7	9		1	0	3	3	4	4	5		2·9
8	10		0	0	4	12		4	2		3·2
9	8			2	0	2		3	1		1·6
10				0	3	6		4	3		1·6
11				0	1	2		1	2		0·6
12						6			1		0·7
13						4			2		0·6
14						1			2		0·3
15						1					0·1
Total	111	52	10	10	36	81	44	35	47	39	46·5
Life	9	3	8	11	11	15	7	11	14	4	9·3

Total issues   = 46·5
Life   = 9·3
Av issues/yr = 46·5/9·3
           = 5·0

The average circulation curve for this group of books can be obtained from the averages for each year. Note that when the book is withdrawn its circulation is zero and this zero circulation must be taken into account when calculating the average. This average circulation curve in shown in the right-hand column of the table.

The total issues for each book can be obtained by summing the annual circulation figures. The average total issues for the category can be obtained either by summing the average annual issues, that is, the right-hand column, or by taking the average of the total issues of each book.

Underneath the column for each book we can also put the life, that is, the age of the book when it is withdrawn. The average of these figures is the average life of a book in the category.

The average annual circulation for books in the category can be obtained by dividing the average total issues for the books by the life of the category. In the example in Table 5, average annual circulation is 5·0.

This method works fairly well if we carried out a survey of withdrawn books. In fact, it is the best method for examining circulation curves in detail. However, it does have some shortcomings and in particular it is biased because it cannot allow for the effect of those books that are withdrawn involuntary, ie pilfered or lost.

To allow for such books it is necessary to make some independent assessment of the rate at which these losses occur. This loss rate can then be used to correct the total issues and the average life of the books by using the following two empirical formulae:

% correction for total issues = 0·66 × life × % annual loss rate
% correction for life   = 0·50 × life × % annual loss rate

For example, if we assume that 1 per cent of the stock is lost each year we have in our example to apply these two corrections:

% correction for total issues = 0·66 × 9·3 × 1 = 6·2%
% correction for life   = 0·50 × 9·3 × 1 = 4·7%

Therefore,

corrected total issues   = 46·5 (1− 0·062) = 43·6
corrected life   = 9·3 (1 − 0·047) = 8·9
corrected average annual issues = 43·6/8·9 = 4·9

In the overall picture these corrections are unlikely to be significant unless the loss rate of books is high.

If we have not carried out a survey of withdrawn books, then the circulation parameters can still be estimated from data drawn from surveys of shelf stock and returned books.

In this case we need to make two assumptions. The first concerns the life of the books and the second concerns the average annual issues of the books over their lifetime.

If the age profile of the books in a category is uniform and if all the books in the category are withdrawn after the same life, then it is evident that the average age of the books will be a half of the life. Transposing this relationship we get:

Life = 2 × Average age

This relationship becomes only approximate if the age profile of the books is not even or if they are not all withdrawn after the same life. Nevertheless, in the absence of any other data it is a sufficiently good approximation to work with.

The second relationship also depends on an even age profile and uniform life of books within a category. This relationship states that the average annual circulation of the average book in a category over its lifetime is equal to the average annual circulation of all books in the category at any particular time. This latter can be found simply by dividing issues per year from the category by the stock in the category. Thus we have:

$$\text{Average annual circulation of a book} = \frac{\text{Total issues/year}}{\text{Total stock}}$$

The total issues of the average book in the category over its lifetime can be obtained from the average life and the average annual issues by the following relationship:

Total issues per book = Average issues per year × Life

Applying these relationships to our illustration we get:

Age	= 3·08 years
Issues per year	= 2310
Stock	= 218
Life	= 3·08 × 2 = 6·16
Average issues per year per book	= 2310/218 = 10·60
Total issues per book	= 10·60 × 6·16 = 65

Replacement

If the librarian has been carrying out a regular policy of withdrawal linked to a regular programme of replacement, then clearly for the stock to remain constant in size the rate

Table 6 The data matrix

Category	Stock	Is/yr	Age	Bk ln	Bk sh	Pr ln	I/Y/B	Life	Tot I	Rep R
1 Bus St	237	2020	2·09	112	125	0·472	8·52	4·18	36	57
2 Relig	321	2805	5·52	155	166	0·484	8·74	11·04	96	29
3 Homes	476	4160	3·36	230	246	0·484	8·74	6·72	59	71
4 Food	218	2310	3·08	128	90	0·587	10·60	6·16	65	35
5 Medic	136	1193	5·47	66	70	0·486	8·77	10·94	96	12
6 Garden	268	2436	5·95	135	133	0·503	9·09	11·90	108	23
7 Transp	376	3465	3·98	192	184	0·510	9·22	7·96	73	47
8 Railway	179	2089	4·68	116	63	0·646	11·67	9·36	109	19
9 Soc Sc	525	3480	4·05	193	332	0·367	6·63	8·10	54	65
10 Science	90	400	3·59	22	68	0·246	4·44	7·18	32	13
11 Country	391	4381	4·89	243	148	0·620	11·20	9·78	110	40
12 Animals	251	2467	4·71	137	114	0·544	9·83	9·42	93	27
13 Sport	506	4098	4·06	227	279	0·448	8·10	8·12	66	62
14 Art	509	2764	4·86	153	356	0·301	5·43	9·72	53	52
15 Music	226	1870	3·55	104	122	0·458	8·27	7·10	59	32
16 Photo	126	1425	2·37	79	47	0·626	11·31	4·74	54	27
17 Biog	804	8842	7·49	490	314	0·609	11·00	14·98	165	54
18 Lit	370	2493	5·42	138	232	0·373	6·74	10·84	73	34
19 Milit	426	4426	5·15	245	181	0·575	10·39	10·30	107	41
20 Geog	840	5714	6·95	316	524	0·377	6·80	13·90	95	60
21 Hist	672	5233	6·19	290	382	0·431	7·79	12·38	96	54
22 Misc	264	1241	4·41	69	195	0·260	4·70	8·82	41	30
Sub total	8211	69312	5·09	3838	4373	0·467	8·44	10·17	86	884

23 Gen Fic	3391	38976	5·71	1835	1556	0·541	11·49	11·42	131	297
24 Mystery	1220	22508	3·86	1059	161	0·868	18·45	7·72	142	158
25 Romance	503	9105	2·98	429	74	0·852	18·10	5·96	108	84
26 Western	124	1231	3·31	58	66	0·467	9·93	6·62	66	19
27 Sci Fi	153	1397	5·28	66	87	0·430	9·13	10·56	96	14
28 Hist	938	11262	4·53	530	408	0·565	12·01	9·06	109	104
29 Larg P	1085	17051	2·75	803	282	0·740	15·72	5·50	86	197
30 Short S	123	819	5·41	39	84	0·313	6·66	10·82	72	11
31 Yng Ad	113	710	3·71	33	80	0·296	6·28	7·42	47	15
32 Pap Bk	3094	54403	1·33	2561	533	0·828	17·58	2·66	47	1163
Sub total	10744	157462	3·65	7412	3332	0·690	14·66	7·30	98	2063
Grand total	18955	226774	4·27	11249	7706	0·593	11·96	8·55	93	2947

of withdrawal must equal the rate of replacement. This rate must also remain constant over time so that the quality of the stock remains unchanged and issues are sustained. If these rates are not continued then in the short term the stock will have to work harder to maintain the issues. In the longer term this will affect the quality and availability of the stock and issues will fall.

This replacement and withdrawal rate necessary to maintain issues can be calculated in one of two ways. First, and most obviously, it can be calculated from the following formula:

$$\text{Replacement rate} = \frac{\text{Stock}}{\text{Life}}$$

The other way of calculating the replacement rate is by this formula:

$$\text{Replacement rate} = \frac{\text{Issues per year}}{\text{Total issues per book}}$$

This relationship is saying that we must put back into the library what has been taken out by borrowing.

Both relationships give the same answer and the relationship to use depends on what data are available. We can illustrate both methods using our example:

Stock   = 218
Life   = 6·16
Issues per year   = 2310
Total issues per book   = 65
Replacement rate (1)   = 218/6·16 = 35
Replacement rate (2)   = 2310/65 = 35

These analyses have covered the whole of the data matrix and we can now show the results of the analysis on all categories in the full matrix in Table 6.

This table was produced by using a spreadsheet analysis program on a microcomputer. With this method the results can be obtained literally at the touch of a button and changed as easily. Obviously this is the best way of taking the work out of the analysis but it is important that the basic relationships underlying the matrix are fully understood before proceeding with interpretation of the results and then using the results to evaluate policy.

Chapter Eleven

Interpretation

The purpose of this chapter is twofold. First, we will show how the information in the data matrix can be interpreted. Second, we will introduce the idea of targeting. Our interpretation of the output will be done under four headings: demand, supply, book performance and policy.

Demand
We argued at length in chapter 3 that a measure of demand is the number of people interested in reading a book. We showed how this was related to the probability that a book is on loan. Demand for a category of books, therefore, is related to the proportion of books on loan in the cateogory. This is not a direct linear relationship but something more complex. Nevertheless, it can be used to rank categories of books in order of demand. So if we look at Table 6 we will find that there is a much greater demand for Mystery and Romance than there is for Art and Science books.

In interpreting the data in this way we are making a number of assumptions about the nature of the books in the category. In particular we assume that the books in the category are reasonably homogeneous, that is, there are the same number of people (but not necessarily the same people) interested in each book in the category. If categories are defined such that they contain a mixture of books with high demand and books with low demand, then the proportion on loan becomes meaningless as a measure of demand.

It is possible to conduct a deeper investigation into the probability of books being on loan. This probability can be calculated for individual books by using the relationship:

Probability
of book be- = $\dfrac{\text{Annual issues of book} \times \text{Average loan period}}{365}$
ing on loan

This relationship states that the probability of a book being
on loan is equal to the proportion of time it spends on loan.

A distribution of these probabilities can be worked up
from the data by calculating them for each book and applying the sample factors. Thus, a table is built up as follows:

Probability	No of books	% of total
0·0 − 0·1	10	2
0·1 − 0·2	22	5
0·2 − 0·3	58	14
0·3 − 0·4	101	24
0·4 − 0·5	64	15
0·5 − 0·6	73	17
0·6 − 0·7	51	12
0·7 − 0·8	22	5
0·8 − 0·9	10	2
0·9 − 1·0	11	3
	422	100

And this table is graphed as shown in Figure 6.

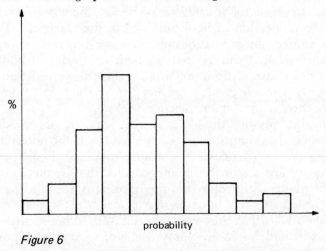

%

probability

Figure 6

It would be too much to hope that each book in a category
has the same annual circulation and hence the same probability. Nevertheless, we would like most of the books to

have a probability that clusters fairly evenly about a single maximum as in the example. If this is not the case, it may be necessary to split the category and rework the data.

Supply
The supply of books in a particular category is measured simply by the number of books on the shelf. Note that it is the books on the shelf that are important and not the total stock. The borrower is unaware of the size of the stock when choosing books. What the borrower sees is the books on the shelf and this is the supply. One problem with high-demand books is that with a high proportion on loan it requires a very large total stock to ensure that there is a reasonable size stock on the shelf. This problem is well illustrated by the Romance category in our example, with only 74 books on the shelf despite a total stock size of 503.

Book performance
The performance of a book is measured by its life and the total issues it will achieve in that lifetime. In our example we have calculated these parameters indirectly from data obtained from surveys of shelf stock and returned books. They were based on assumptions that the age profile of the books is fairly uniform and parameters such as annual issues and replacement rates remain constant over time. However, if this is not the case, then these results must be treated with some suspicion. Let us illustrate some of the problems that can occur when an unstable situation occurs due to a reduction in the level of replacement.

Let us suppose we have a group of books with a total stock size of 1,000 supporting 15,000 issues per year. Books are withdrawn from stock after a lifetime of five years. The age profile of the books initially is uniform, so 200 books are withdrawn each year as they reach the end of their lives. However, at some point the decision is taken to replace books at the rate of only 100 per year. The year-by-year implications of this are shown in Table 7.

It has been assumed in producing this table that the annual issues remain constant. The first point to notice is that the average age of the books does not remain at the level of half the book's life during the transition period. More seriously, however, the issues per book rise and at Year 3 and beyond

Table 7

Age of book (yrs)	No of books in each age bracket in successive years					
	0	1	2	3	4	5
0–1	200	100	100	100	100	100
1–2	200	200	100	100	100	100
2–3	200	200	200	100	100	100
3–4	200	200	200	200	100	100
4–5	200	200	200	200	200	100
Total stock	1000	900	800	700	600	500
Average age (yrs)	2·5	2·7	2·9	2·9	2·8	2·5
Issues/year/book	15·0	16·7	18·8	21·4	25·0	30·0
Total issues/book	75	90	109	124	140	150

reach impossibly high levels. That is, they exceed the maximum level that can be achieved with all books spending no time on the shelf. When this happens the only solution is for issues to collapse. In fact, issues would start to decline even earlier in the process because the quality of choice as evidenced by the shelf stock would be declining. The example also presupposes that each book has an indefinite life in terms of the number of issues that it can support. This is clearly not the case and it is debatable as to whether an average book can sustain more than 100 issues over its lifetime. What would then happen is that the older books would get withdrawn early, before reaching an age of five years. This would reduce the stock still further and increased pressure on the remaining stock would lead to a further reduction in issues.

The approximations for life and total issues/book both tend to substantiate the current replacement policies in the library, even when these policies are insufficient to support the current level of issues. This unstable situation can be detected from the data when a high total issues/book is coupled with a high annual issues per book.

In these circumstances it is necessary to carry out further analysis so that a more reliable picture can be built up. The existing data can be analysed to produce an age profile for the category. This will indicate any instability in replacement historically. It would be very useful at this point to carry out a survey of withdrawn books so that a more accurate picture of book performance can be built up.

By contrast we may also find there are books in the library with low predicted total issues. Although we can decide to reduce total issues by withdrawing books from a library early the converse is not necessarily true. Books with a short life or low total issues may be that way because there is a very limited demand for them. Leaving these books on the shelf indefinitely will not yield any more issues from them.

In summary, therefore, it may be necessary to analyse book performance data further and correct some of the information in the data matrix. When we have done this we can rework the replacement rates. These new figures will be the replacement rates necessary to maintain stock and issues at their current level. Withdrawal rates must of course equal replacement rates for stability. We may not be happy with existing stock and issues levels and may wish to change them. This leads us on to the concept of targeting.

Policy

There are two areas in which it is possible to set policy targets. These are book performance and supply. Book performance has already been discussed in this chapter. What this chapter suggests is that the category-by-category evidence should be viewed and suitable targets set for book life and total issues within that life. These will then be used as a basis for reworking the data matrix.

Ideally a target of 80-100 issues for hardbacks and 30-40 issues for paperbacks should be set, the former to be achieved in five to seven years and the latter in three years. However, analysis of the evidence may suggest that these targets are not achievable simply because the demand is not there. Some categories of books may lose their currency after a relatively short period and should therefore be replaced by more topical material. Failure to do this may lead to issues from the old stock with borrowers taking it in the absence of anything better but the librarian may not be satisfied with this. One of the effects of financial cutbacks will be the need to carry on getting issues out of an ageing bookstock because there are not the funds for replacement. This will be reflected in longer target lives and greater target total issues.

Targeting the shelf stock and, therefore, the supply of books gets to the very heart of librarianship and the management of the library system. Much will depend on the objec-

tives that have been set. In a categorized library the aim is to
provide an easily assimilated choice to the borrower. This is
achieved by breaking the bookstock down into a limited
number of categories from which the choice may be made.
Within each category a range of choice should be provided.
This range should be sufficiently large but not so large as to
be overwhelming. This suggests that the categories should be
designated very carefully. Once designated the aim should be
to provide approximately equal numbers of books on the
shelf in each category.

At this point a clearer distinction must be made between
the categories used for survey purposes and the categories that
may be used for the purposes of displaying books on the shelves.
The need for this distinction can be illustrated by two examples.
Both refer to the data matrix at the end of the last chapter.

The first example concerns the General Fiction category.
In the library being surveyed some fiction is displayed in
genre groupings (eg Romance, Mystery, etc) whilst other
fiction is shelved by author under the heading 'General
Fiction'. It has been decided to split this large group into
three separate categories. It was not possible to adopt this
split for the purposes of survey because such a classification
of data was beyond the abilities of the survey assistant.
Nevertheless, in the absence of such survey information it is
possible to assume that each of the sub-categories had the
same book performance characteristics as the General Fiction
category. It is necessary to make some estimate of the
number of books in each of the sub-categories. As we have
assumed that the characteristics of the sub-categories are the
same we can assume that the total stock splits between the
sub-categories in the same proportions as the shelf stock.
It will be necessary, therefore, only to carry out a quick
survey of the shelf stock so that it can be apportioned.

This process can be used to rebuild the data matrix as
shown in Table 8. This table was produced by:
1 Transcribing the proportion on loan, issues/year/book,
  life and total issues figures from the General Fiction
  category.
2 Writing in the books on the shelf from the secondary survey.
3 Apportioning total stock, and issues/year according to
  the proportions of shelf stock.
4 Recalculating books on loan and replacement rates.

Table 8

Category	Stock	Pr ln	Bk ln	Bk sh	Is/yr	I/Y/B	Life	Tot Is	Rep R
GFI	1116	0·541	604	512	12825	11·49	11·42	131	97·7
GF2	1395	0·541	705	640	16031	11·49	11·42	131	122·1
GF3	880	0·541	476	404	10120	11·49	11·42	131	77·1
Totals/avs	3391	0·541	1835	1556	38976	11·49	11·42	131	296·9

Table 9

Format	Stock	Pr ln	Bk ln	Bk sh	Is/yr	I/Y/B	Life	Tot Is	Rep R
PB	470	0·828	389	81	8268	17·58	2·66	46·8	176·7
HB	503	0·852	429	74	9105	18·10	5·96	107·8	84·5
Totals/avs	973	0·841	818	155	17373	17·85	4·36	77·9	261·2

The second example concerned the paperback category. In fact, books in this category are shelved both as a separate group and together with other categories, notably the fiction groupings such as Romance and Mystery. It was anticipated that the performance characteristics of all paperbacks was similar for the purposes of survey. Nevertheless we wish to combine hardbacks and paperbacks in the sâme display category and to this end we wish to deal with them as a single category in the data matrix. The technique for doing this is the same as above. That is, the paperback category is split into component categories using information obtained from a supplementary survey if necessary. The paperback sub-categories are then added on to the appropriate hardback category to obtain a combined display category.

This process is illustrated in Table 9 using the Romance category as an example. It can be seen from this example that the replacement rate obtained by adding the values for the two sub-categories is different from that obtained by applying either of the two formulae to the data in the bottom line. This occurs because the formulae assume that all the books in a category are homogenous — that is, have approximately the same life and the same total issues within that life. When this is not so, as in the case of a mixture of paperbacks and hardbacks, then the formula will give only an approximation. Where such an obvious split occurs in a category it is good practice to do as we have done here, that is, split the category into its components, survey each separately and build up the replacement rates from the sum of the component rates.

Once we have designated the display categories in this way and reworked the data matrix we can set targets for the shelf stock within each category. We might aim for a library containing 40 categories of books each with a shelf stock of 250 books. To achieve shelf stock targets of this nature will involve removing or injecting stock to achieve the required choice on the shelf.

In a more traditional library in which books are shelved either by author or in Dewey order the policy will probably be to maintain a representative range of choice over the whole spectrum of fiction and non-fiction. However, even in these libraries it is from the shelf stock not the total stock that the borrower or the librarian selects books. Therefore it will be necessary to decide on the size of the shelf stock necessary to present an acceptable range of choice.

One interesting point that emerges from this discussion is that the range of choice offered at a library is dependent on the shelf stock and this could be quite independent of library size expressed in terms of the number of borrowers it serves. Therefore, in theory a library with a shelf stock of 10,000 books provides the same standard of service whether it serves 1,000 or 10,000 borrowers. Of course, the total stock necessary to provide this shelf stock will be very different in each case.

Summary
In summary this chapter has shown how to look critically at the data matrix produced at the end of the previous chapter. The first step is to be satisfied that the information it contains is satisfactory and valid. This is especially true in the area of book performance. It may be necessary to conduct further analysis and survey before the data matrix is acceptable. Then the new matrix can be interpreted to draw conclusions about demand for various categories of books, the state of the supply and the performance and potential of bookstock currently in the library. Replacement rates necessary to maintain the demand should also be noted. With this information policy targets should be set principally in relation to book supply, that is, the number of books on the shelf. These targets may involve re-categorizing the bookstock as well as changing stock levels. In the next chapter we will use these targets and show how they can be used to formulate a number of policies.

Chapter Twelve

Stock injection

Bookstock policies fall into two groups. In the first are those immediate policies involving restructuring of the bookstock. In the second group are those ongoing policies that are necessary to maintain stock and issues.

Before discussing these policy options it would be useful to summarize the position we have reached in the analysis. We have surveyed the existing bookstock and we have obtained a detailed picture of how it is used category by category. This picture includes a measure of the demand for each category (proportion out on loan), the supply of books in each category (the shelf stock) and the performance of the books (life, total issues). We have already started to look at the policy implications of maintaining the status quo by replacing books at a suitable rate. We have looked at the problems of re-categorizing the bookstock where the existing method of shelving books is unsatisfactory and needs to be changed. On the basis of this information we have set some performance targets for the bookstock and we have also set targets for the supply or the shelf stock. This chapter will discuss how these supply targets can be met and maintained.

In an existing library there will be two problems with the supply of books. In some categories the replacement rate will not have kept pace with the demand for books and heavy borrowing will have resulted in a small selection of books on the shelf from which a large number of people have to choose. In this case it will be necessary to provide a better choice of books by injecting stock into the category.

The second problem is the converse of this. This occurs where there is a wealth of published material in categories which are in low demand. Here the shelf stock may be far greater than that necessary to provide a range of choice for the small number of borrowers. This overstocking can also occur because the shelf stock contains 'dead' books which, although they have achieved relatively few issues, are no longer circulating. Overstocking can be cured by weeding books from the shelf and hence presenting a smaller choice to the borrower. The techniques for evaluating both stock injection and wholesale stock withdrawal are the same. In what follows we will discuss the techniques for evaluating stock injection.

The purpose of stock injection is to ensure that shelf stock targets are met. Thus, if the current shelf stock is, say, 150 books and the target shelf stock is 250 it is necessary to inject stock so that the target is reached. Obviously it is necessary to inject more than 100 books because new books will only spend a proportion of their time on the shelf. In order to find the amount of stock that needs to be injected to achieve the necessary shelf stock it is necessary to have some idea of the effect of stock injection on the issues.

There are three hypotheses that form the basis for a relationship between changes of stock and changes in issues. Each of these hypotheses may be appropriate in different circumstances. We will deal with each in turn.

The first hypothesis is that injection of stock into a category has no effect on issues outside that category. In other words the new stock is borrowed by existing borrowers in the category or by new readers coming into the library. The second hypothesis is that injection of stock into a category has no effect on the total issues of the library but there is some transfer between categories such that borrowers move from a number of categories to the category into which stock has been injected. The third hypothesis is really an embellishment of the second, in which we assume that as well as a transfer of borrowing between categories there is also an increase in issues. This is caused by existing borrowers using the library more or by new borrowers coming into the library.

We can work through each of these hypotheses by means of an example. We will use the Mystery category as an illustration without necessarily implying that any particular hypotheses fits this category.

First, we assume that injection of stock into one category has no effect on the other categories. We then assume that the injected stock behaves in exactly the same way as the existing stock. Thus the new stock will have the same life and total issues/book as the existing stock. If this is the case then the issues/year/book will remain the same. The issues will go up at the same rate as the stock increase. The number of books on loan, which is directly related to issues, will go up at the same rate and hence the shelf stock will increase at the same rate as the total stock. Thus, knowing the desired increase in shelf stock we can work backwards and rebuild the line in the data matrix.

This process is illustrated in Table 10. The table was built up as follows:

1 The appropriate line was copied from the data matrix into the 'Before' row.

2 The target shelf stock was copied into the 'After' row under the number of books on the shelf.

3 A factor was calcuated by dividing the target shelf stock by the initial shelf stock. In this example the value of the factor was 250/161 or 1·55.

4 The factor was used to multiply Stock, No of books on loan and Issues/year from the 'Before' row to obtain the appropriate values in the 'After' row.

5 The proportion on loan, issues/year/book, life and potential issues of the book, all of which remain unchanged, are copied from the 'Before' row to the 'After' row.

6 The replacement rate is calculated using the appropriate formula.

7 The increases in stock, shelf stock, annual issues and replacement rate are calculated by subtraction.

The table shows that to increase the shelf stock by 89 books from 161 to 250 an injection of 674 books must be made which will lead to annual issues from the category increasing by 12,442 to 34,950.

This hypothesis can be refined in two ways. First, it is quite probable that injecting stock into a category will lead to diminishing returns. In other words, some of the pressure will be removed from the existing stock and none of the stock in the category will have to work quite so hard. Thus, issues/year/book will decrease after injection and this will lead to a less than proportionate increase in issues. This in turn will mean that rather fewer books need to be injected to achieve the required shelf stock target. On the other hand we have

Table 10

	Stock	Pr In	Bk ln	Bk sh	Is/yr	I/Y/B	Life	Tot Is	Rep R
Before	1220	0·868	1059	161	22508	18·45	7·72	142	157·9
After	1894	0·868	1644	250	34950	18·45	7·72	142	245·2
Increase	674			89	12442				87·3

Table 11

	Stock	Pr In	Bk ln	Bk sh	Is/yr	I/Y/B	Life	Tot Is	Rep R
Before	1220	0·868	1059	161	22508	18·45	7·72	142	157·9
Hyp 1	1894	0·868	1644	250	34950	18·45	7·72	142	245·2
Hyp 2	1894	0·823	1558	336	33132	17·49	7·72	135	245·2

seen when we examined circulation curves in earlier chapters that the circulation of a book is higher when new. Thus, if we inject brand-new books we would expect these books to have a higher rate of issues than existing stock. It follows, therefore, that injecting new books may lead to a more than proportionate increase in issues and hence we may need to inject even more books to achieve the shelf stock target.

The interaction between these two factors is complex and will vary over time. In the short term they may cancel out and in the longer term shifting patterns of demand will vary all relationships anyway. Perhaps the best assumption to make in initial analysis is the simple assumption we made at the beginning, namely that the injected stock behaves in the same way as the existing stock. We will return to this variability in later chapters when we discuss monitoring.

One further point worth noting in this example is the replacement rate. In the short term there will be no increase in replacement rate and the increase shown in this example will only become necessary as the new injected stock reaches replacement age.

In the previous hypothesis the issues from the library increased solely as a result of more people borrowing from a single category. Issues from all other categories remained unchanged. This may not be a realistic hypothesis in those cases where there is transferability between categories. One simple way of modelling this transferability is to take the initial data matrix, inject stock into one of the categories and re-calculate the issues from that category by using the first hypothesis, namely issues will increase proportionately to stock. Then reapportion all issues between categories so that total issues remain unchanged.

This reapportionment process is demonstrated in Table 11. This table was built up as follows:

1 The first two rows were derived exactly as described for the first hypothesis.

2 A factor was derived to scale down the annual issues in all categories so that the total annual issues from the library remained the same. This factor was calculated by dividing the total annual issues from the library by that total plus the additional issues in this category caused by the stock injection. In this example the value of the factor was $226,774/(226,774 + 12,442)$ which equals 0.948.

3 This factor was used to multiply the issues/year and the books on loan in the second row to get the appropriate values in the third row.

4 The stock and average life of the books which remain unchanged are copied from the second row to the third row.

5 The proportion on loan, number of books on the shelf, issues/year/book, potential issues and replacement rate are all calculated using the appropriate formulae.

It will be seen from this example that as a result of the redistribution of issues, books in this category (and all other categories) are working less hard. This means that our injection of 672 books in this category has led to an increase in shelf stock of 175 overshooting the target by some 86 books.

In order to multiply up the shelf stock by a factor of 336/161 or 2·09 we have to multiply up the total stock by only 1894/1220 or 1·55. In fact, we wish to multiply up the shelf stock only by a factor of 1·55 so that it reaches its target of 250. To find the increase in total stock necessary to reach this target we can approximate to the answer by calculating a multiplication factor for total stock that is equal to the square root of the multiplication factor for the shelf stock. In this example the multiplication factor for the total stock is the square root of 1·55 or 1·24.

We can use this factor to rebuild the table (Table 12). We can see that the square root formula is only an approximation. Nevertheless, it gives us a reasonably acceptable answer.

This example also illustrates nicely the two-stage process involved in increasing shelf stock. In the first stage the shelf stock is increased by injection of stock. In the second stage the new issues generated by the injection are redistributed taking some of the pressure off books in this category and thus further increasing the shelf stock.

Using this hypothesis we only need to inject a stock of 293 books into this category to achieve the target shelf stock of 231 books. Issues in the category will rise by 4,753 to 27,261 with a corresponding fall in issues in all other categories.

So far our estimates of the stock injection necessary to achieve our shelf stock target range from 293 to 674 with an increase in library issues ranging from 0 to 12,442. In practice there is most likely to be both an increase in total library

Table 12

	Stock	Pr ln	Bk ln	Bk sh	Is/yr	I/Y/B	Life	Tot Is	Rep R
Before	1220	0·868	1059	161	22508	18·45	7·72	142	157·9
Hyp 1	1513	0·868	1313	200	27910	18·45	7·72	142	195·9
Hyp 2	1513	0·847	1282	231	27261	18·02	7·72	139	195·9
Increase	293		223	70	4753				

Table 13

	Stock	Pr ln	Bk ln	Bk sh	Is/yr	I/Y/B	Life	Tot Is	Rep R
Before	1220	0·868	1059	161	22508	18·45	7·72	142	157·9
Hyp 1	1708	0·868	1483	225	31511	18·45	7·72	142	221·1
Hyp 3	1708	0·868	1464	244	31110	18·21	7·72	140	221·1

issues and a redistribution of issues as a result of injecting stock into one category. The necessary stock injection will be between the two values given above, and the resulting increase in library issues will also lie between the above two values. This compromise represents hypothesis 3. The technique for calculating the stock injection is identical to that used for hypothesis 2, except that an additional factor needs to be included to account for the new stock necessary to support the additional issues. We can calculate a multiplying factor to represent the amount by which issues are expected to rise. This factor is then multiplied by the factor for the shelf stock increase, and a factor for the total stock increase is found by taking the square root of the product of the two component factors.

This can be illustrated by an example. We take the same category with the same target shelf stock as before but assume that the total annual issues will rise by 6,000. This gives a factor for the issues of (22,508 + 6,000)/22,508 or 1·27. The factor for total stock will be the square root of 1·27 × 1·55 or 1·40 and this new factor can be used to produce Table 13 using exactly the same technique as was used for hypothesis 2.

Theoretically, hypothesis 3 is saying that if stock injection in one category leads to a redistribution of issues from all categories then the shelf stock in all categories will increase. This increase in shelf stock presents the borrower with a wider choice and is thus an improvement in the quality of the library. This improvement in quality will over time lead to an increase in library issues.

In obtaining a factor for the effect of the stock injection on issues we have used the issues from that category to obtain a multiplication factor. It can be seen that hypothesis 1 is merely a special case of hypothesis 3 in which the issues from the category will go up in the same proportion as the required increase in shelf stock. Thus, to return to our initial example, the shelf stock is multiplied by a factor of 1·55 and we have assumed issues from the category to be multiplied by the same amount. Total stock will therefore need to be multiplied by a factor equal to the square root of 1·55 × 1·55 which is 1·55.

In practice we will wish to inject stock into or withdraw stock from several categories simultaneously. We can investigate such wholesale restructuring of the book stock by adopting the following procedure. This procedure is illustrated by Tables 14 and 15.

Stage 1:

1 For each category list the existing stock, the existing shelf stock and the target shelf stock.

2 Calculate a multiplication factor for shelf stock by dividing the target shelf stock by the existing shelf stock.

3 Specify a multiplication factor to model the effect of the injection in each category on the quality of the library as reflected in a change of issues. This will lie between 1 and the factor obtained in the previous step. In the example we have chosen a value midway between these two extremes.

4 Obtain a multiplication factor for stock by multiplying the two factors above and taking the square root.

Stage 2:

5 Use this factor to obtain the new stock level.

6 Calculate the injection of stock by subtracting the existing stock from the new stock.

7 List the existing annual issues (1) by category.

8 Make a first estimate of the new annual issues (2) by multiplying the existing annual issues by the factor obtained in step 4.

9 Total up the new annual issues by category to obtain a first estimate of the total annual issues from the library.

10 Decide what the total annual issues from the library will be after the restructuring. This can be done by multiplying existing annual issues (1) by category by the factor obtained in step 3 and summing to obtain the grand total. In this example we have chosen to believe the effects in the various categories will cancel out and total issues will remain unchanged.

11 Reapportion the issues obtained in step 9 so that they sum to the required total (3).

12 Calculate the new shelf stock. This is done in the example by subtracting the books on loan from the new stock. The books on loan have been calculated by multiplying the annual issues by the loan period and dividing by 365.

13 Work out the discrepancy between the new shelf stock and the target shelf stock.

Table 14 Evaluating multiple injections, Stage 1

Category		Stock	Exist Bk sh	Targt Bk sh	Bk sh M Fac	Is/yr M Fac	Stock M Fac
1	Bus St	237	125	125	1·00	1·00	1·00
2	Relig	321	166	125	0·75	0·88	0:81
3	Homes	476	246	250	1·02	1·01	1·01
4	Food	218	90	125	1·39	1·19	1·29
5	Medic	136	70	125	1·79	1·39	1·58
6	Garden	268	133	250	1·88	1·44	1·64
7	Transp	376	184	125	0·68	0·84	0·75
8	Railway	179	63	125	1·97	1·49	1·71
9	Soc Sc	525	332	250	0·75	0·88	0·81
10	Science	90	68	50	0·74	0·87	0·80
11	Country	391	148	125	0·84	0·92	0·88
12	Animals	251	114	125	1·09	1·05	1·07
13	Sport	506	279	250	0·90	0·95	0·92
14	Art	509	356	125	0·35	0·68	0·49
15	Music	226	122	125	1·02	1·01	1·02
16	Photo	126	47	75	1·59	1·30	1·44
17	Biog	804	314	500	1·59	1·30	1·44
18	Lit	370	232	125	0·54	0·77	0·64
19	Milit	426	181	250	1·38	1·19	1·28
20	Geog	840	524	500	0·95	0·98	0·97
21	Hist	672	382	250	0·65	0·83	0·74
22	Misc	264	195	75	0·38	0·69	0·52
Sub total		8211	4373	4075	0·93	0·97	0·95
23	Gen Fic	3391	1556	1000	0·64	0·82	0·73
24	Mystery	1220	161	250	1·56	1·28	1·41
25	Romance	503	74	250	3·36	2·18	2·71
26	Western	124	66	75	1·14	1·07	1·10
27	Sci Fi	153	87	75	0·86	0·93	0·89
28	Hist	938	408	500	1·23	1·11	1·17
29	Large P	1085	282	250	0·89	0·94	0·91
30	Short S	123	84	125	1·48	1·24	1·35
31	Yng Ad	113	80	75	0·94	0·97	0·96
32	Pap Bk	3094	533	750	1·41	1·20	1·30
Sub total		10744	3332	3350	1·01	1·00	1·00
Grand total		18955	7706	7425	0·96	0·98	0·97

Table 15   Evaluating multiple injections, Stage 2

Category	New Stock	Stock Injct	Is/yr (1)	Is/yr (2)	Is/yr (3)	New Bk sh	Error
1 Bus St	237	0	2020	2018	2075	122	−3
2 Relig	261	−60	2805	2282	2346	131	6
3 Homes	482	6	4160	4215	4334	242	−8
4 Food	281	63	2310	2973	3056	111	−14
5 Medic	215	79	1193	1883	1936	107	−18
6 Garden	441	173	2436	4005	4117	213	−37
7 Transp	284	−92	3465	2616	2689	135	10
8 Railway	307	128	2089	3579	3679	103	−22
9 Soc Sc	426	−99	3480	2825	2905	265	15
10 Science	72	−18	400	320	329	54	4
11 Country	344	−47	4381	3859	3967	125	0
12 Animals	268	17	2467	2638	2712	118	−7
13 Sport	466	−40	4098	3776	3882	251	1
14 Art	248	−261	2764	1346	1384	171	46
15 Music	230	4	1870	1899	1953	121	−4
16 Photo	181	55	1425	2047	2105	64	−11
17 Biog	1154	350	8842	12690	13046	431	−69
18 Lit	238	−132	2493	1605	1650	147	22
19 Milit	546	120	4426	5678	5837	223	−27
20 Geog	812	−28	5714	5520	5676	497	−3
21 Hist	494	−178	5233	3849	3957	275	25
22 Misc	136	−128	1241	640	658	100	25
Sub total	8123	−88	69312	65758	67607	4009	−66

23	Gen Fic	2463	−928	38976	28312	29108	1093	93
24	Mystery	1721	501	22508	31754	32647	185	−65
25	Romance	1361	858	9105	24632	25324	169	−81
26	Western	137	13	1231	1355	1393	71	−4
27	Sci Fi	137	−16	1397	1249	1284	76	1
28	Hist	1096	158	11262	13153	13523	459	−41
29	Large P	991	−94	17051	15575	16013	237	−13
30	Short S	167	44	819	1110	1141	113	−12
31	Yng Ad	108	−5	710	679	698	75	0
32	Pap Bk	4024	930	54403	70764	72754	600	−150
	Sub total	12204	1460	157462	158082	162528	3078	−272
	Grand total	20327	1372	226774	220571	226773	7087	−338

14 If this discrepancy is unacceptably large — and it will be if there are major changes made in some categories — it may be necessary to repeat the process with the new stock levels.

When an acceptable answer has been reached the data can then be fed back into the full data matrix.

In this chapter we have discussed ways of evaluating the targets set in the previous chapter. In particular we have discussed ways of evaluating stock injection and weeding policy as a means of achieving shelf stock targets. There are other policy issues concerned with the placement of books in different libraries which we will discuss in the next chapter. The policies necessary to maintain targets that have been reached by stock injection and the institution of rotating collections will be discussed in chapter 14.

Chapter 13

Bookstock rotation

Up to this point in the book we have looked at bookstock in relation to a single library. However, most public lending libraries are part of wider systems containing a number of branch libraries of very different sizes and characteristics. Thus, what is good or valid for one library in terms of bookstock policy is not necessarily good for another. To analyse the differences between libraries we have to return to the basic principles of book circulation.

When we examined book circulation in earlier chapters we noted that the circulation of a book was related to the size of the library in which it was placed as measured by the annual issues from that library. Using this concept we can draw up theoretical circulation curves for the same book in

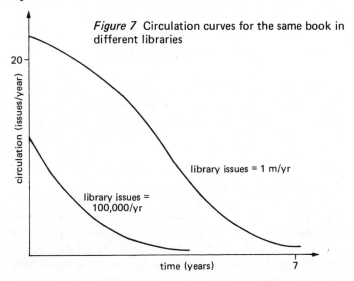

Figure 7 Circulation curves for the same book in different libraries

two libraries of different sizes. These curves are shown in Figure 7.

The total issues of the book over its lifetime are found by measuring the area under each of the curves. So from the graph we can see that in the larger library the book will achieve 80 issues over its lifetime of seven years and in the smaller library it will achieve only 30 issues over its lifetime of five years. This relationship between library size and total issues of a book can be generalized across the whole range of library sizes and a graph can be plotted as shown in Figure 8.

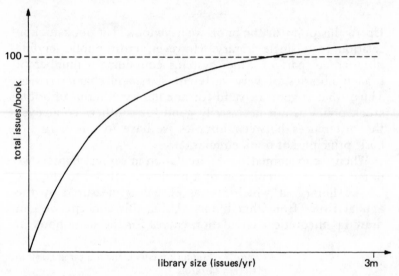

Figure 8 Total issues/book against library size

This shows the total issues of a book will increase with library size although at a decreasing rate. In theory this increase in total issues will go on indefinitely. In practice, we have already found that there is a limit to the number of issues that can be obtained for any book before it loses its topicality or falls apart. This ceiling to total issues is also shown on the graph.

So much for the relationship between book circulation and library size but there is also a relationship between book circulation and library quality. That is, the larger the range of choice (or shelf stock) from which borrowers are able to choose, the less likely they are to borrow a particular book and therefore the smaller will be its circulation. The converse is also true, that as the choice of stock becomes more restricted then the higher becomes the circulation of individual books within the stock. Thus, if we were to measure the actual circulation over time of the same title in a number of libraries of different sizes we would find a relationship rather different from the one plotted above. This is because librarians will tend to provide a more restricted choice in the smaller library and a wider choice in larger libraries. What the graph above represents is the effect of trying to provide the same quality of choice in libraries of different sizes.

The total issues of existing books can be translated into the concept of potential issues of new books. Thus, if we were considering whether to acquire a particular new book for a library we would be interested in the potential issues of the book over its lifetime. By dividing the acquisition costs of a book by the number of potential issues we can obtain an acquisition cost/issue for a book in libraries of different sizes. This transformation has been carried out using the graph in Figure 8 and an acquisition cost/book of £8. The result is shown in Figure 9.

This graph shows well the exorbitantly high costs of providing a service in the smaller library. To overcome this

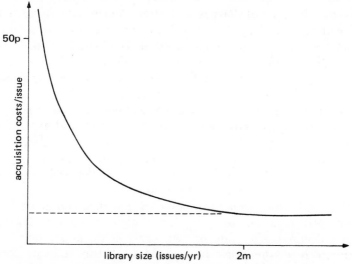

Figure 9 Relationship between acquisition costs and library size

problem three possible solutions can be adopted. The first of these has already been discussed. A more restricted choice can be provided in the smaller library, thus making the stock work harder, forcing up the total issues of the books and so reducing the cost/issue. This technique is one which is commonly used, though perhaps subconsciously, by librarians. However, it does have its limitations. There comes a point when the choice of books is so restricted that potential borrowers find it not worthwhile to use the library for that particular subject. Thus, rather than increasing total issues the reverse might happen.

The second solution is rather more extreme. This involves simply not trying to provide for low-interest subjects in small libraries. Thus, as part of the analysis process described in previous chapters, a policy decision could be taken to weed out those categories with low total issues and provide a partial library service consisting only of the more popular material.

There is a third solution worth considering and that is to provide for low-interest categories using collections of books that move between libraries. In the rest of this chapter we will discuss techniques for evaluating such rotating collections.

Book circulation is a function of the number of people interested in a book. Circulation declines with time for two reasons. First, people have read the book and are not interested in reading it again and, second, people lose interest in the book because it is no longer topical. Bookstock rotation is especially appropriate where the decline in circulation of a book in a library is due to the first reason, that is, the book having been borrowed by all those interested in it. The theory is that if the circulation has declined for this reason it can be revived by moving it to another library and exposing it to a new group of borrowers who may not have read it.

Candidates for bookstock rotation have to be selected with care. Typically they will be non-fiction books with a small but enthusiastic and patient readership.

If we take the circulation curve of a typical candidate for bookstock rotation we will see a high initial circulation which declines after one or two years as those people who wish to read the book have done so. After four or five years the circulation will have declined to such a level that the book is sitting on the shelf practically all the time and at this point it should be withdrawn. The total issues that the book will have achieved over its lifetime may be as low as 20-40. This circulation curve is illustrated in Figure 10.

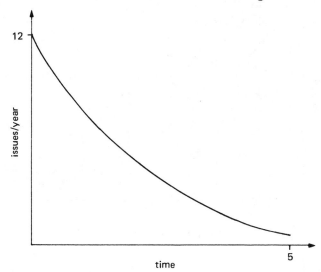

Figure 10 Circulation curve

If we were to move this book after a year we would expect to see a revival of circulation. If we continued to move this book annually we would hope to see a continual revival in circulation each year. In theory, with some books this process could be carried on indefinitely but again practical limits should be placed on the process as the book will lose its topicality after a period of time and will in any case start to fall apart after a certain number of issues. Nevertheless, with this process it should be possible to double or even treble the total issues to be obtained out of the book. The process of issue revival is illustrated in Figure 11.

Each time a book is moved the total issues to be obtained out of the book are increased. This relationship between number of moves and total issues can be plotted in the form of a graph, as in Figure 12.

It is no coincidence that this graph is similar to the one showing the relationship between total issues and library size. Bookstock rotation in fact ensures that a book is exposed to a greater and greater catchment of borrowers. Indeed, one way of obtaining a plot of total issues against

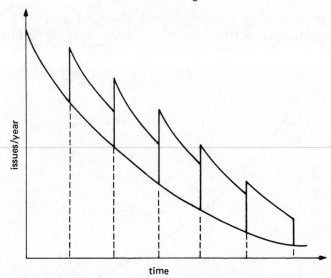

Figure 11 Issue revival with bookstock rotation

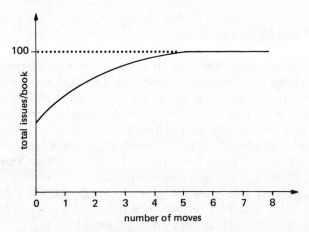

Figure 12 The effect of book movement on total issues

number of moves is to transpose the theoretical curve of total issues against library size.

This curve of total issues against number of moves together with the acquisition cost of a book can be used to plot a curve of acquisition cost/issue against number of moves. This curve is shown in Figure 13.

There is a penalty attached to moving books between

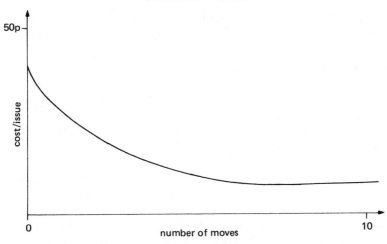

Figure 13 Acquisition costs against number of moves

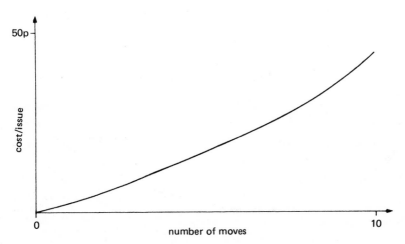

Figure 14 Transport costs against number of moves

libraries in the form of increased administration and transport costs. These costs will be proportionate to the number of book movements taking place. By multiplying the unit transport cost of a book movement by the number of moves and dividing by the total issues linked to that number of moves, it is possible to obtain a relationship between transport costs/issue and the number of moves. This relationship is shown in Figure 14.

The two graphs of acquisition costs/issues against number of moves and transport costs/issue against number of moves can be combined to give the total cost/issue against number of moves. This combination is shown in the graph in Figure 15.

It can be seen from this graph that there is a clear minimum. This minimum will usually occur at a point near to where transport costs are equal to the acquisition costs. So if acquisition costs/book are £8 and transport costs/book/move are £2 then the acquisition costs equal transport costs at four moves and this will represent the optimum. It can be seen from the graph that there is a 'kink' in the graph of acquisition costs where the total issues reaches its maximum and further movement of the book will not achieve any further issues. If this kink occurs at a number of moves lower than the value calculated above then this will be the optimum. Thus, the best policy is to move a book until the amount spent on transport is equal to the acquisition cost or until it reaches its maximum issues, whichever represents the fewer moves.

Another useful feature of the minimum cost is that the trough in the graph is fairly flat about the minimum. This means that the number of moves is not absolutely critical.

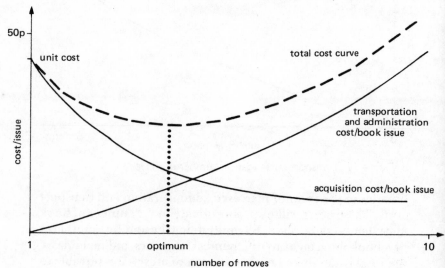

Figure 15 Total costs against number of moves

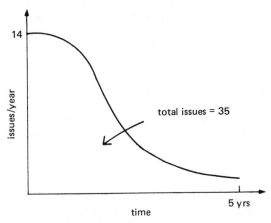

Figure 16 Circulation curve of a candidate for bookstock rotation

Let us now draw together all these ideas in an example. We have a book with a circulation curve as shown in Figure 16. The first year's issues of the book are 14 and then the circulation declines fairly rapidly over a period of five years, when it is withdrawn. The total issues over this period are 35. We estimate that the acquisition cost of the book is £8 and the cost of moving it between libraries will be £1.50 per move. The most economic number of moves will be about five. We estimate that this circulation policy will extend the life of the book to six years. Thus, in order to achieve five moves in this period the book must be moved once every year.

With this policy we would anticipate that the book will achieve more than the 35 issues it achieved without moving from the library. However, it would be unlikely that even with circulation it will continue to achieve 14 issues each year over its lifetime. The actual total issues will lie somewhere in the range 35 to 84. For the purposes of subsequent analysis we have assumed that it will achieve a total issue of 72 over its lifetime of six years. That is an average of 12 issues per year.

With this information we are now in a position to return to our familiar data matrix and work out the effects of bookstock rotation. In Table 16 we have two rows. The first row shows the effect of placing that book and a number of similar books in the library without any bookstock rotation.

The second row shows the same category achieving the same issues with bookstock rotation. In the second row of the

Table 16

	Stock	Pr ln	Bk ln	Bk sh	Is/yr	I/Y/B	Life	Tot Is	Rep R
Without	200	0·39	78	122	1400	7·0	5·0	35·0	40
With	117	0·67	78	39	1400	12·0	1·0	12·5	117

table the life of the books is given as one year because that is the time the books spend in the library. The replacement rate is the rate at which books come into the library from outside. Because the entire stock moves annually the replacement rate is the same as the size of the stock. However, on average only 1/6 of this stock will be new books and, therefore, the replacement rate of new books will be 19·5. If we look at the shelf stock with bookstock rotation we can see that it is considerably less than without rotation. Indeed, the objective of circulating collections is to provide a choice to the borrower not by providing a large number of relatively static books on the shelf but with a smaller number of books with a high turnover rate.

The above analysis was based on an assumption about transport costs that was literally plucked out of the air. Suppose the transport costs were considerably lower than the costs we have assumed. Theoretically this would mean that we could move the books between libraries even faster with profit. There are two practical considerations militating against this. First, it is unlikely, especially with the extra wear and tear involved in stock rotation, that the book will achieve many more than 72 issues before it is withdrawn no matter how frequently it is moved. Second, we have assumed that books can be moved instantaneously between libraries. In fact this is not so and there will be a certain loss of issues due to loss of availability of the book while it is being transferred. If the number of transfers are too frequent this loss of issues will become significant and cancel out any gains from the rotation of the bookstock.

This analysis shows that, provided the right books are selected for rotation, it is a worthwhile policy. The policy should operate within certain limits. The life of the book should not be extended beyond the point at which it is no longer topical or it falls to pieces. The frequency with which the book is moved should be sufficient to make it worthwhile but not excessive. In practice most bookstock rotation policies will involve moving books at between one- and two-year intervals. Provided these limitations are accepted, bookstock rotation is worth embarking upon without too much prior analysis but its progress should be monitored carefully and policy reviewed at intervals.

We have discussed the implications of a low transport cost but it is also important for a successful bookstock rotation policy to avoid high transport and administration costs. The practical issues involved in bookstock rotation become important. Costs will rise significantly if elaborate catalogues are maintained of rotating collections showing the current location of each book in the collection. Even with computer technology it can be a resource-consuming process to record a change of location each time a book is moved. For this reason catalogues for rotating collections should not show location and in some cases should be dispensed with altogether.

The analysis has also assumed that the rotating collection is moving between libraries of approximately equal size. It could be that if one of the libraries is smaller than the rest, the issues from the book could actually fall below the level it would have achieved had it remained in one of the larger libraries. This may not necessarily be a bad thing if this is the only way that the smaller library can get books on a particular subject. The other choice open is to split the rotating collection so that it goes from one medium library to two smaller libraries, thus providing a more restricted choice at the smaller libraries and thus forcing the books to work harder.

There are a number of schemes for managing rotating collections, two of which are described here. The first is the 'cascade', and the second is the 'merry-go-round'.

The cascade involves acquiring the collection new for a large library in the system and then, after a period of time, splitting it into a number of smaller collections, each of which move to smaller libraries and so on down the line. The problem with this system is that there will be reluctance for the larger library to relinquish the collection until it is worked out there. This will mean that the smaller libraries in the system will be receiving very secondhand material. Arguably this is better than no material at all but it is far from satisfactory. To overcome this some systems inject new stock into the cascade at various points. This certainly freshens up the collection but the newly injected stock will only have a short and uneconomic lifespan. The cascade does have the advantage that it is easily controlled and managed.

The merry-go-round involves libraries of approximately equal size moving books between themselves in a continuous circle. Thus, in our example we would have a circle of six libraries. Each library would replace a sixth of the collection before shelving it. Each year the collection would move from each library in the circle to the next one along. Thus, in theory each library would receive its fair share of new books. The age profile of the collection in each library would remain uniform. Smaller libraries can be accommodated in the circle by inserting them in parallel with the collection being split as it enters these libraries and reassembled as it leaves. The merry-go-round is simple and effective. However, it does have a number of organizational implications which will be discussed later.

With both systems it is necessary to identify books as being part of a rotating collection. This can easily be achieved with some distinguishing mark on the book jacket. There will be a tendency to move the collection as a unit. However, if this is done there will be a period of time in each library when the collection is being assembled and to do this books have to be withdrawn from circulation. This has an adverse effect on the issues achieved from the stock. This problem can be overcome by moving those books that are due for a move as soon as they become available. With books that are on the shelf this presents no problem. With those books on loan the transfer process may last several weeks as the books are returned. This is not difficult to manage provided a regular transport service exists between libraries in the chain.

These practical details are the matter of some discussion between librarians and will continue to be so for a number of years. It is not the purpose of this book to enter this debate but rather to provide a theoretical background in which this discussion can take place. It is to be hoped, however, that this chapter will convince those librarians who are not already convinced of the merits of bookstock rotation as a means of reducing costs whilst maintaining levels of service. Although the practical difficulties are not insignificant, they can be overcome in a way that ensures that this policy meets its objectives.

Chapter 14

Stock replacement

In the previous two chapters we have looked at one-off policies of restructuring the library in various ways so that it meets the targets that have been set for it. At the end of this process we can produce a data matrix with the new stock, issue and book performance data. This information can be processed to calculate a replacement rate necessary to maintain the library in its new condition.

For the library to remain stable the rate at which books are replaced must be the same as the rate at which they are withdrawn. It may be that the withdrawal rates are also subject to policy. That is, it may have been decided, for example, to reduce the age of the bookstock by withdrawing books earlier. This policy objective will have been built into the data in targeting book performance. Thus, the replacement rates shown in the final data matrix will be those necessary to attain all the policy objectives.

Although it is relatively easy to set targets of book life and total issues it may not be so easy to achieve them in practice. Therefore, it will be necessary to monitor stocks carefully to ensure that stock levels are being maintained so that withdrawal or replacement rates can be adjusted as necessary. This process of monitoring is discussed in more detail later.

There is a short cut to this analysis process which is valid especially in categorized libraries. We have already suggested that in these libraries the objective will be to maintain a limited number of categories and within each category to present a shelf stock of a particular size. These parameters will be built into the design of the library; thus there will be a number of shelving bays, one or more bays assigned to each category and each bay or group of bays having a capacity that is equal to the target shelf stock. Once this system is set up and the shelves are stocked with books it is simply necessary to withdraw books as and when required and to fill the resulting gaps in the shelves with replacement books. The self-regulating nature of categorized libraries has long been appreciated and understood by librarians. Nevertheless, although buying books by the metre is a simple procedure it is necessary to carry out the analysis described above as a planning exercise so that appropriate budgets can be set. If the analysis is correct then the replacement rate produced by it will be the same as the rate necessary to fill the gaps in the shelves.

We have described the principles of replacement but how can these principles be applied in practice? At present books are selected by librarians who scan publishers' lists at regular intervals and make a selection from these lists within resource constraints. This process must now be embellished in two ways. First, in addition to the overall quota of books implied by the resource constraints there will be individual quotas for particular categories. The second involves an assessment of the contribution that an individual new book will make to the library.

When we discussed book performance one of the most important parameters we measured was the total issues that a book achieved over its lifetime. We have seen that this parameter is a direct determinant of the replacement rate, as this rate can be calculated by dividing the annual issues from the category by the total issues per book. Even in the most homogeneous categories of books the total issues will not be the same for each title. It should be possible as part of the analysis to investigate this variation within a category and to attribute it to some independent measure or measures of the book such as treatment, format and so on. In principle this concept of total issues of existing books can be applied to new books in the form of potential issues.

One job that the librarian must do then, whilst scanning the publishers' lists, is to make some sort of estimate of the potential issues of each title. With this estimate the librarian will then acquire books in each category so that the sum of the potential issues acquired is equal to the annual issues from that category. Clearly the most cost-effective way of achieving a replacement policy is to select those books with the highest number of potential issues per pound sterling. In practice this procedure will not be adhered to rigorously and in any case there are all sorts of difficulties in making accurate assessments of the potential issues of new books. Nevertheless, as more data are collected and analysed the librarian should obtain a better feel for the type of books that should be selected to make best use of limited resources.

Now let us touch briefly on the problem of purchasing duplicate titles. If two copies of the same title are acquired for a library then the potential issues obtained from that title are not doubled. In fact, the effect of having duplicates in a library can be modelled using the theoretical model of circulation developed in chapter 3. This will show that potential issues are only increased by about 50 per cent on acquisition of the second copy, and third and subsequent copies will yield relatively small increases in potential issues. Thus duplicate buying is only justified if the second copy of a popular title will increase potential issues more than the least popular book in the category being purchased. This is likely to occur when there is a wide variation within a category and a limited choice of material.

The process of stock replacement along the lines above can be formalized by the procedure described and illustrated below.

In this example the books on offer from publishers in a particular category are listed together with their prices. An

Category: Geography
Issues/year: 5714

Title	Cost(£)	Pot Is	Cost/Is	Rank
1	8·00	60	0·13	10
2	7·50	90	0·08	4
3	3·00	30	0·10	6
4	6·00	120	0·05	1
5	10·00	100	0·10	6
6	8·00	90	0·09	5
7	3·00	40	0·08	3
8	8·00	80	0·10	6
9	12·00	120	0·10	6
10	7·00	100	0·07	2

estimate is made for each book as to its potential issues and a cost/issue is derived by dividing the cost of the book by its potential issues. Books are then ranked by their cost/issue.

Annual issues from this category are 5714 so the total potential issues acquired in any one month should be 1/12th of this or 476. We then arrange books in their rank order and work out the cumulative potential issues as in Table 17.

Table 17

Title	Rank	Pot Is	Cum Pot I
4	1	120	120
10	2	100	220
7	3	40	260
2	4	90	350
6	5	90	440
3	6	30	470
5	6	100	570
8	6	80	650
9	6	120	770
1	10	60	830

From this we can see that we obtain the required potential issues at minimum cost by acquiring the first six ranked books on the list, that is, titles 4, 10, 7, 2, 6 and 3.

If we were to get two copies of the first ranked book then we estimate that the potential issues from both copies will be 180, that is an increase of 60. The marginal cost/issue of the extra copy is £0.10. This is the same as the cost/issue of the sixth ranked book. Therefore, it does not matter whether we get two copies of title number 4 or one copy of this title and one copy of title number 3.

With this technique the librarian is buying potential issues rather than books. The number of books bought will depend on what is on offer in the form of new books. The average performance of new books may be different from that of the existing stock and for that reason the actual replacement rates may be different from those calculated in the data matrix. Constant monitoring should ensure that eventually the performance characteristics used for calculation purposes reflect the effects of replacement policy. Monitoring is discussed in the next chapter.

Chapter Fifteen

Monitoring

The techniques described in previous chapters have been set up in response to the need to reorganize libraries to serve the users better. The emphasis has, therefore, been on the idea of a one-off review. We have envisaged a survey to gather information, an analysis of that information and a formulation of policies, some of which involve restructuring the bookstock. Once the library has been got into shape by this process it is important that it is kept in this state.

Much of the information collected as part of our survey will have been imprecise. Moreover, in order to evaluate policy options we have had to make some sweeping assumpttions. Neither of these factors should inhibit us from making changes in the library. Nevertheless, there is a need to review the decisions made in the light of their subsequent effects to ensure that they continue to meet their objectives.

The process of monitoring consists of two parts. On the one hand it is necessary to refine some of the data that we have used, especially in those areas where the initial estimates were imprecise due to inadequate samples or other factors. On the other hand, and perhaps more importantly, we need to measure the effects of the various policies we have introduced, for example, stock injection or bookstock rotation, to ensure that they continue to meet the objectives and targets set for them.

There are two areas in which data refinement can be carried out usefully. The first of these is the average loan period. We saw that when we came to calculate the number of books on loan in each category the loan period data that we had was too inaccurate to be used. This inaccuracy was due to samples of returned books that were insufficient. We

therefore had to make do with the average loan periods for
larger groups of books (fiction and non-fiction) to calculate
the number of books on loan by category.

The average loan period will vary between categories and
is of interest in itself. It is also vital to know the number of
books on loan at any time. These parameters are related and
it is necessary to get a better estimate of one or the other
of them.

If a better estimate of loan periods can be obtained by, for
example, continually surveying returned books, then the
books on loan by category can be obtained by the formula

$$\text{Books on loan} = \frac{\text{Issues/year} \times \text{Loan period}}{365}$$

If a better estimate of books on loan by category can be
obtained directly from the issuing system then loan periods
by category can be calculated from the formula

$$\text{Loan period} = \frac{\text{Books on loan} \times 365}{\text{Issues/year}}$$

If a figure for books on loan is collected directly it must be
corrected in two ways. First, it must be averaged out to
allow for the variation that occurs on a day-by-day basis.
Second, allowance must be made for book losses. Books that
have not been returned after some time must either be
collected in some way or written off.

When an accurate and up-to-date picture has been obtained
of the number of books on loan it can be added to the number of books on the shelf to give the total stock in each
category. An up-to-date picture of shelf stock can be
obtained by regular counts of the books on the shelves. When
this accurate measure of total stock is compared with one
obtained by traditional methods, ie updating a base figure
with withdrawals and acquisitions, an estimate will be obtained
of losses from both books issued but not returned and books
leaving the library without being issued.

Stocktaking for rotating collections is much easier. When a
library receives a rotating collection a count can be made of
it on reception. Withdrawals can then be subtracted from this
count and additions to the collection can be added. After
the collection has been introduced into the library a count
can be made of the shelf stock and this can be subtracted

from the total stock to give an independent estimate of the number of books on loan. When the collection is ready to move on to the next library in the chain an inventory can be taken again of the number of books in the collection. This can be used to estimate the loss rate of stock whilst in the library. The loss rate, spread over the period that the book was in the library, can be used to correct the estimates made of total stock and stock on loan.

With small categories of books the stock on loan and the stock on the shelf will vary quite considerably from day to day. We are not interested in this variation for analysis purposes but instead we are trying to build up a static picture of the state of the library. To achieve this it might be necessary to take the average of a number of consecutive weekly counts.

In formulating and evaluating policies for stock injection and bookstock rotation a number of heroic assumptions have been made about the effect of these policies on the issues. These assumptions must be checked once the policies have been implemented. Moreover, especially in the case of stock injection, it is not just the issues in the category involved that will be affected but it may well be issues across all categories. Therefore, it is necessary to keep a regular check of the rate of issues by category for all categories of books in the library. Fortunately issues are already monitored by librarians so techniques already exist. These techniques must be adapted to measure issues by category of book.

Throughout the analysis we have seen the importance of book performance data, that is, all the information related to the circulation curve of a book: its issues year by year, its life and the total issues achieved over its lifetime. This information can be built up over time by continually surveying withdrawn books as they become available. The techniques for doing this have been described in an earlier chapter.

This technique of building up historical patterns of book performance and using them as a basis for policy is valid provided both the category of books and the library in which that category is situated have remained stable over a period of time. However, if the category has been the subject of some policy change, then this is likely to lead to instant changes in the annual issues which will distort the pattern of the circulation curve. A more immediate and more accurate technique for measuring book performance is to collect information from books currently in use. For this technique to be successful a fairly large sample of books is required. For this reason the technique is best restricted to those categories of book where major changes in policy require detailed monitoring information.

In theory the circulation of the book in its nth year of life is the same as the circulation of a book n years old. Thus, if we have a group of books of different ages it should be possible to draw up an average circulation curve by using the last year's circulation of each book and plotting this figure on a graph of issues against age. The line drawn through these points will be a proxy for the circulation curve of an average book in the category.

In practice there are two main problems to this approach. First, it is likely that the variation in circulation between books of the same age is greater than the circulation of the average book at different ages. Because of this variation we need a relatively large sample of books of each age in order to make a reliable estimate of the average circulation of each age group. In some extreme cases a 100 per cent sample of the books in a category may not be sufficient.

The second problem concerns withdrawn books. In making an estimate of the average circulation of a book of a particular age we need to allow for books in the sample that have been withdrawn and therefore have a zero circulation. Thus, if we survey a 100 per cent sample of 50 four-year-old books we need to know the total number of books that were acquired for the library four years ago. Thus, if there were 80 such books acquired our estimate of the average circulation of a four-year-old book must be reduced to allow for 30 books with a zero circulation.

This can be illustrated by a worked example:

Number of books surveyed	= 50
Average circulation of books surveyed	= 12 issues/year
Number of books acquired	= 80
Number of books withdrawn before survey	= 30

$$\text{Corrected average circulation} = \frac{50 \times 12 \times 30 \times 0}{80}$$

$$= 7.5 \text{ issues/year}$$

Although we can build up a picture of the performance of bookstock by surveying the current stock at regular intervals we still need historical data on acquisitions by category. It may take some time to build up this information.

The principal problem with monitoring book performance is the estimation of the life of books. Even in those libraries where target lives have been set for different categories the actual life will be different for two reasons. First, there will be involuntary withdrawals due to loss and pilfering which do not adhere to the targets. Second, it is difficult in practice to withdraw the books at a precise moment in time. What actually happens is that books are withdrawn on the basis of a series of subjective criteria such as condition, topicality and current issue rate, and the target life merely provides a framework for this process.

Perhaps the best compromise for monitoring book performance is to use a hybrid technique in which information from both withdrawn stock and current stock is combined. With this technique withdrawn books are surveyed to obtain the age of the book at withdrawal — its life — and this is combined with the average annual issues of the current bookstock to get an estimate of the total issues of books by category. The average annual issues of the current bookstock is obtained easily by dividing the annual issues for the category by the total stock in the category.

The performance of books in rotating collections can be measured easily. The life of the book is simply the time it spends in the library and this will be defined by policy. The average annual issues of a book can be calculated as described above. The total issues of a book can be found from combining these two pieces of information.

We have already discussed the need to measure replacement and withdrawal rates by category as a means to monitoring other areas of data. However, these data are also worth monitoring in their own right. Withdrawal and replacement will be the subject of policy targets but it is necessary to measure actual rates to ensure that targets are being maintained. A system should therefore be set up to record the number of withdrawals and replacements by category at regular intervals.

In summary this chapter has suggested that in order to improve the initial estimates and monitor the effects of policy it is necessary to keep on a regularly updated basis the following information by category of book.

1 Number of books on the shelf.
2 Number of books on loan or loan period.
3 Rate of issues.
4 Life of books currently being withdrawn.
5 Withdrawal rates.
6 Replacement rates.

Most of this information can be obtained with any issuing system although it will require some ingenuity to record issues by category with a token system. The monitoring process can be made much easier by making use of a computerized issuing system. Unfortunately, many computerized issuing systems have been designed badly to fulfil the single objective of replacing a manual system. To take full advantage of a computerized system it is necessary to build into it the ability to produce regular management information of the type described above.

To analyse policy effectively we need historical information. Some of this information will be obtained by carrying out the surveys described in earlier chapters. However, some information such as replacement rates by category of book over time will not be available. It is therefore vital that monitoring policy is formulated and implemented at the earliest possible stage, ideally even before the surveys have been carried out. In other words it is too late to wait until surveys are carried out, policies formulated and implemented before thinking about the need to monitor the effects of policy. In the extreme, if a policy is going to be a disaster, the sooner we know about it the better.

Chapter Sixteen

Organizational implications

Practising librarians who have done any work on systematic bookstock management usually hold some central function in the library system. From this one may be forgiven for thinking that a centralized library system is a prerequisite of systematic bookstock management. In illustrating the ideas in this book with examples drawn from a single library we have gone some way to dispelling this idea. Nevertheless, it is unlikely that a branch librarian will have sufficient time left from his duties in running the library to spend much time carrying out the sort of research necessary to restructure it. Much of the initial work will therefore be carried out by headquarters staff with few day-to-day administrative duties and, therefore, more time to devote to longer-term strategic issues.

There are two phases in library management. The first phase is the analysis, formulation of policy, introduction of new systems, restructuring of the bookstock etc. The second phase is the continuing operation, within the constraints and to meet the targets set by the first phase. Inevitably, work in the first phase will fall to central staff, who can take one library in the system at a time and reorganize it before moving on to the next. However, the second phase can, with profit, be delegated to the local level and if this is to be done there is much to be said for involving the·local librarian in the first phase.

First then, we need a full-time team of librarians whose job it is to go into individual libraries and restructure them. This team will go into a library, survey the library thoroughly and analyse the data. They will then make decisions about the way that the books ought to be shelved, the number of categories, the size of each category, and the implications of these targets for weeding stock out and injecting stock. They will decide which of the stock to place in rotating collections and how these collections should be organized. Incidentally, the need to manage rotating collections efficiently may conflict with existing divisional structure and this structure may have to be reviewed.

When the library has been restructured in this way it will then be passed over to another group who will be responsible for maintaining the library within the constraints and the targets set by the restructuring process. Usually this responsibility will devolve to the branch librarian, but in a number of library authorities libraries are managed by non-professional library managers and the continuous maintenance and professional support of libraries is carried out by their headquarters team. Whichever system is adopted, however, there will be a group of people responsible for the ongoing maintenance of the library. This person, or group of people, will have two main responsibilities. First, there is the day-to-day running of the library into which should be introduced the need to monitor information carefully. Thus, there will be the issuing of books and the handling and shelving of returns. There will be the constant reshelving of shelf stock together with other duties not directly connected with the borrowing side of the library, such as providing an information service.

The other responsibility, however, will be the responsibility for withdrawing books and acquiring replacement stock. As we have shown in an earlier chapter, this operation will be based round a category-by-category quota of books that has been drawn up on the basis of analysis. Both the analysis and the subsequent monitoring of withdrawal and replacement policy, together with the updating of replacement quotas, should be the job of the central team. However, there is a lot to be said for allowing branch librarians with their local knowledge to be responsible for replacement policy within their own libraries. If the branch library happens to be a categorized one then again, as we have shown, there may be no need for elaborate analytical techniques to determine the correct replacement rates; the librarian can simply be left to fill the gaps in the shelves by the appropriate new books.

The management of rotating collections presents particular problems. It may seem that there is no reason why the branch librarian should not be responsible for weeding and replacement of books in these collections. However, there are two dangers to this approach. The first danger is that the librarian may purchase for the collection books that are already in it but not due to arrive at the library until some time in the future. The second danger is that two branch librarians, acting independently, might acquire the same book for the same collection. Both of these practices would detract seriously from the value of managing books in this way. One way of preventing this duplication of resources is to centralize the responsibility for managing rotating collections. Thus if a collection were to rotate amongst six branch libraries, these six libraries would form a division and the divisional librarian could be responsible for maintaining the collection. Someone from division would visit each of the branch libraries, weed out stock and replace with new books so that there was no duplication. It would also be the responsibility of the divisional librarian to maintain a catalogue of the rotating collection if one were deemed necessary. A useful compromise alternative which keeps the branch librarian involved is for the divisional librarian to be responsible for buying the appropriate quota of new books for the rotating collection and then making them available for the various branch librarians involved to choose from in order to replenish their stocks.

In summary, therefore, we suggest that the appropriate organizational structure for a public library system is a three-tier one. Centrally, at headquarters, there will be a team responsible for reclassification and restructuring of libraries wihin the system, setting up rotating collections and setting quotas and other guidelines for the maintenance of the system. Librarians at divisional level would be responsible for some aspects of the operation of rotating collections, and branch librarians, in addition to their day-to-day responsibilities for running the library, would also be responsible for book replacement.

Chapter Seventeen

A cookbook

The purpose of this chapter is to summarize the methodology described in chapters 7 to 15. It is intended as a quick source of reference, so no arguments, explanations or alternatives are given. For a fuller discussion the previous chapters must be read.

1 **Preliminary assessment** (chapter 7)
a Examine the library to find:
  — How books are classified.
  — How books are shelved.
  — The issuing system in use.
  — Maximum loan periods.
b Find from existing records and tabulate in as much detail as possible:
  — The existing stock in the library.
  — The shelf stock.
  — The stock on loan.
  — Annual issues.
  — Replacement/withdrawal rates.

2 **Survey design** (chapter 8)
a Categories
  — Split the bookstock into a number of categories (30 to 40) for the purposes of survey.
  — Designate these categories in a way that makes them easily recognizable by a survey assistant.
b Sample size
  — Set a quota for the number of current books to be surveyed with 30 to 40 categories. Aim to get at least 50 books in each category. So go for a sample of at least 2,000 books.

— Sample sizes for withdrawn books will depend on availability. Aim to get as many as possible and stop surveying when stable results are obtained.
— Make an estimate of proportion of books on loan.
— Split the current book survey quota into quotas for the shelf stock survey and the returned books survey.
— Express the quota for the shelf stock survey as a sampling rate.

c Questionnaire design
— Design a survey form with space for the following information:

Heading:
Location
Date
Type of survey (Shelf, Returns, etc)
Name of survey assistant
Sequence number
Book classification:
Category
Dewey number
Format
Level
Etc.
Issues/year
Last year
All previous years of the life of the book
Date of addition to stock or date of first issue
Date due back for survey of returned books only

3 Survey (chapter 8)
a Shelf stock
— Use the 1 in n sampling rate calculated above.
— Find a convenient starting-point.
— Generate a random number between 1 and n (m).
— Take out the mth book from the starting-point.
— Survey the book and return it.
— Count the nth book from the one just surveyed and survey that book.
— Go systematically through the shelves in this fashion until the library is covered.
b Returned books
— Take the books after they have been discharged but

before they are shelved.
- If you cannot survey all the books as they are returned do not bias the sample, ie always take the next available trolley-load.
- Carry out the survey at different times of the day and days of the week.
- Stop the survey when the quota has been reached.

c Withdrawn books
- Ensure the collection is not biased.
- Survey the whole collection provided it does not exceed 2,000, say.
- If it does exceed this amount take a random sample.

4 **Assembling the data** (chapter 9)
a Sample rates
- Shelf stock sample rate is already defined.
- If you have an accurate estimate of stock on loan, use it to calculate the sample rate for books on loan.
- Otherwise process the returned books survey to obtain an estimate of the average loan period from the date of the last stamp.
- Get issues/year from the preliminary assessment.
- Calculate books on loan by the following formula:

$$\text{Books on loan} = \frac{\text{Issues/year} \times \text{Loan period}}{365}$$

- Calculate a sample factor for returned books by using the formula:

$$\text{Sample factor} = \frac{\text{Total books on loan}}{\text{Number of returned books surveyed}}$$

b Stock by category
- Take the books on the shelf and the returned books surveys and carry out a count of the books in each category surveyed in each survey.
- Calculate the stock in each category by the formula:
Stock by category = (Number of shelf stock in category surveyed × Shelf stock sample factor) + (Number of returned books in category surveyed × Returned books sample factor)

c Issues/year
- Take the record of each book surveyed and count

the number of issues in the previous year.
- Tabulate this information by type of survey and by category.
- Calculate the issues/year by category by the formula:
Issues/year by category = (Issues/year in shelf stock surveyed × Shelf stock sample factor) + (Issues/year in returned books survey × Returned books sample factor)

d   Average age of stock
- Calculate the age of each book surveyed by subtracting the date of acquisition from the date of survey.
- Tabulate the cumulative age by type of survey and by category.
- Calculate a cumulative age by category by using the following formula:
Cumulative age by category = (Cumulative age of shelf stock surveyed × Sample factor for shelf stock) + (Cumulative age of returned books surveyed × Sample factor for returned books)
- Calculate average age by category by dividing cumulative age by category by stock by category.

e   Preliminary tabulation
- Produce a table showing for each category of books:
Stock
Annual issues
Average age

5 **Analysis** (chapter 10)
a   Produce a table by category of book with the following headings:
- Stock
- Issues/year
- Age
- Books on loan
- Books on shelf
- Proportion on loan
- Issues/year/book
- Life
- Total issues of a book
- Replacement rate
b   Calculate data for each heading by category using the following formulae:

$$\left.\begin{array}{l} - \text{Stock} \\ - \text{Issues/year} \\ - \text{Age} \end{array}\right\} \text{Given}$$

$$- \text{Books on loan} = \frac{\text{Issues/year} \times \text{Loan period}}{365}$$

$$- \text{Books on shelf} = \text{Stock} - \text{Books on loan}$$

$$- \text{Proportion on loan} = \frac{\text{Books on loan}}{\text{Stock}}$$

$$- \text{Issues/year/book} = \frac{\text{Issues/year}}{\text{Stock}}$$

$$- \text{Life} = 2 \times \text{Age}$$

$$- \text{Total issues of a book} = \text{Issues/year/book} \times \text{Life}$$

$$- \text{Replacement rate} = \frac{\text{Stock}}{\text{Life}} \text{ or } \frac{\text{Issues/year}}{\text{Total issues/book}}$$

c Withdrawn books
  - Tabulate the data with one table for each category of book which shows for each book in the category the annual issues over its lifetime.
  - Note the life of each book.
  - Find an average circulation curve for each category by taking the average circulation for each year of life. Do not forget to account for the zeros.
  - Find the average total issues/book by adding up the average circulation curve.
  - Correct the total issues/book for losses by applying the following formula:
    % correction = 0·66 × life × % annual loss rate
  - Find the average life by taking the average of the life of each book in the category.
  - Correct the average life for losses by applying the following formula:
    % correction = 0·5 × life × % annual loss rate
  - Calculate the average annual issues of a book by dividing average total issues by average life.

6 Interpretation (chapter 11)
a Book performance
  - Check performance characteristics generated by both

the survey of current books and the survey of withdrawn books.

— Set targets for life and/or total issues for those categories where existing levels are too high.

— Insert new book performance characteristics.

b Categorization of bookstock

— Examine each survey category in turn and decide
whether survey categories are suitable as display
categories.

— Split categories that are too large into smaller sub-
categories by estimating distribution of total stock on
the basis of shelf stock distribution.

— Amalgamate categories that are too small.

— Re-present the data matrix with reworked display
categories.

c Targeting

— Set targets for the shelf stock in all categories.

— Select categories for rotating collections and set
targets for annual issues in these categories.

7 Stock injection (chapter 12)

— For each category list the existing stock, the existing
shelf stock and the target shelf stock.

— Calculate a multiplication factor for shelf stock by
dividing the target shelf stock by the existing shelf
stock.

— Specify a multiplication factor for issues. This will
lie between 1 and the factor obtained in the previous
step.

— Obtain a multiplication factor for stock by multiplying the two factors above and taking the square root.

— Use this factor to obtain the new stock level.

— Calculate the injection of stock by subtracting the
existing stock from the new stock.

— List the existing annual issues by category.

— Make a first estimate of the new annual issues by
multiplying the existing annual issues by the multiplication factor for stock.

— Total up the new annual issues by category to obtain
a first estimate of the total annual issues from the
library.

— Decide what the total annual issues from the library

will be after the restructuring. This can be done by multiplying existing annual issues by category by the multiplication factor for issues and summing to obtain the grand total.

— Reapportion the new annual issues so that they sum to the required total.

— Calculate the new shelf stock by subtracting the books on loan from the new stock. The books on loan have been calculated by multiplying the annual issues by the loan period and dividing by 365.

— Work out the discrepancy between the new shelf stock and the target shelf stock.

— If this discrepancy is unacceptably large it may be necessary to repeat the process with the new stock levels.

— When an acceptable answer has been reached the data can then be fed back into the full data matrix.

8 Bookstock rotation (chapter 13)

a Selection
   — Select categories for rotation between libraries. The books in these categories should be:
      Of specialist interest and hence with low circulation
      Of enduring interest

b Frequency
   — Estimate optimum number of moves by dividing unit replacement cost by unit transport cost.
   — Estimate interval between moves by dividing life by number of moves + 1.
   — Reset interval if less than 1 year and more than 2 years.

c Book performance
   — Estimate new life of books in collection.
   — Set down minimum total issues/book (the present level) and maximum (the new life × first year's issues).
   — Estimate between minimum and maximum total issues/book for books in a rotating collection.

d Evaluation
   — Target the annual issues for each category of the rotating collection in the library.
   — Rework the appropriate rows of the data matrix using target annual issues and book performance measures.

9 Stock replacement (chapter 14)

a Initial review
   - Calculate replacement rates by category by dividing stock by life or annual issues by potential issues/book when data matrix is finalized.
   - Calculate annual budget by multiplying replacement rates by acquisition costs/book.

b Continuing management
   - Set out issue rate by category.
   - Take publishers' lists etc and list titles, and cost, of all new books.
   - Estimate potential issues for each title.
   - Calculate cost/issue for each title.
   - Rank books by cost/issue.
   - Select the top-ranked books so that the cumulative potential issues is equal to the issue rate.
   - Compare cost/issue of multiple copies of the top-ranked book against the least-ranked book selected.

10 Monitoring (chapter 15)

Set up a monitoring process to obtain at regular intervals up-to-date information by category on:
   - Number of books on the shelf.
   - Number of books on loan or loan period.
   - Rate of issues.
   - Life of books currently being withdrawn.
   - Withdrawal rates.
   - Replacement rates.

Index